THE
JESUS
Training Manual

THE JESUS
Training Manual

Operating in
Miracles, Signs,
and Wonders

RICHARD MULL

DESTINY IMAGE® PUBLISHERS, INC.
P.O. Box 310, Shippensburg, PA 17257-0310
"Speaking to the Purposes of God for This Generation and for the Generations to Come."

Previously published as *Lord, Disciple Me* by Destiny Image Publishers
Previous ISBN: 0-7684-2271-X

This book and all other Destiny Image, Revival Press, MercyPlace, Fresh Bread, Destiny Image Fiction, and Treasure House books are available at Christian bookstores and distributors worldwide.

For a U.S. bookstore nearest you, call 1-800-722-6774.
For more information on foreign distributors, call 717-532-3040.
Reach us on the Internet: www.destinyimage.com.

ISBN 13 TP: 978-0-7684-3746-1
ISBN 13 HC: 978-0-7684-3747-8
ISBN 13 LP: 978-0-7684-3748-5
ISBN 13 Ebook: 978-0-7684 9007-7

For Worldwide Distribution, Printed in the U.S.A.
1 2 3 4 5 6 7 8 9 10 11 / 13 12 11

Dedication

There have been a few people who have walked the journey of discipleship described in these pages. These are my closest and most trusted friends. As author John Eldredge has put it, these people have been my platoon. We've fought together, played together, wept together, and often prayed together. They have guarded my back and encouraged me in the face of overwhelming discouragement and adversity. They hung in when it seemed like everyone else ran. The Lord knew I couldn't make the journey into His discipleship program alone, so He gave me a few close friends.

Dawn (Beautiful), my wife, my friend, and my greatest encourager—you have truly walked every step of the journey.

Endorsements

I've known Richard and his ministry for about ten years. His *40-Day Revolution* and *First Strike* were powerful tools at the early Call events. I believe that this book *The Jesus Training Manual* is another powerful resource that is foundational for every believer to become a true disciple of Jesus.

Lou Engle

I was given a copy of *The Jesus Training Manual* at a time when someone very close to me desperately needed a miracle from God. This book gave me comfort that God could really bring freedom and hope, that God could provide the miracle we so needed. I then witnessed firsthand as God healed in answer to prayer. I recommend this book to people everywhere I go.

Jerry Colangelo
Chairman, Phoenix Suns

The Jesus Training Manual shatters conventional wisdom and tells the truth about healing in a postmodern world: the purely "biomedical model" for disease is dead. Medical practitioners all know it but face paltry options. Floundering and disempowered, we watch our American patients spend over $150 billion annually on mostly occult-based "alternative medicine" gimmicks—out of pocket! And many of these gimmicks have the effect of making patients eventually worse! Even the National Institutes of Health, constrained by The American Academy of Science's secular humanist verbiage, admits that nearly two-thirds of patient problems confronted by a primary care physician are psychologically based and underlie psychosomatic signs and symptoms. More precisely, two-thirds of patient problems *are* "psycho-spiritually" rooted. It's time to get past the business of medicine and back to the healing art of medicine. Richard Mull explains how and why and what real healing means in *The Jesus Training Manual*. His is a message I share all day mentoring medical students, while curing, not palliating, "diseased" patients.

Dr. Frank Agnone
Doctor of Internal Medicine
Adjunct Faculty at University of Arizona/ASU Medical School

You continue to have the Lord speak through your writing and change views around the world.

Edward Kobel
President of Departolo Development

I have had the opportunity to read *The Jesus Training Manual* and also witness firsthand the application of these biblical truths. There are many misperceptions and much confusion surrounding the miraculous power of God operating in our world. Richard does a great job of exploring the biblical truths and their application to those in bondage, experiencing spiritual warfare, and brokenness. I encourage you to read this book and go deeper into the Scriptures.

David L. Dunkel
Chairman and CEO Kforce Inc.

Contents

Part II—Biblical Foundations

Foreword

I first read the manuscript of *The Jesus Training Manual* on a flight from Florida to the United Kingdom. My wife and I had just met Richard Mull at a church weekend at South Brandon Worship Center. Richard and his friend, Victor, took us to Tampa airport to catch the plane home. On the way, he told us something of his own pilgrimage and of the impact, completely unknown to me at the time, that the work of Ellel Ministries had already had on his life. He told me about the book and pushed a copy of the manuscript into my hand before we said good-bye at the check-in desk.

As we were taxiing down the runway, I casually flipped through the pages but found myself being drawn into the detail of different parts of Richard's story. This was a real story of a real person who was being unusually honest with himself, his readers, and, most importantly, with God. I turned back to the beginning and started to read from chapter 1. By the time we touched down at London's Heathrow, I had read the whole book! As I read the pages, I felt I had gotten to know the heart of the author and, through his story, understood something more of the heart of God.

The Jesus Training Manual tells the story of Richard's personal pilgrimage from the limitations of his earlier perceptions of "Church" to being gripped by the vision to both be a disciple and then to make disciples. The message that runs through almost every page of the book is one of the most important that today's church needs to hear and understand—that Jesus' instruction to the first disciples to go out and proclaim the Kingdom and make more disciples still holds good for today. Nothing has changed.

But what does it really mean to be a disciple—to fulfill the calling and destiny that God has for you—to live in the dynamic of God's personal anointing for your life? These are vital questions every believer needs to have answered. The first half of the book tells the personal story of how Richard faced up to these critical issues. In the second half, Richard puts it all into the context of the vital scriptural foundations.

Before we landed at London airport, I was recommending the book to my wife. Since then, I have recommended it to all the leaders of Ellel Ministries. And I pray that the recommendation implicit in this Foreword will encourage many more people to read *The Jesus Training Manual* and be as blessed by it as I was!

Peter Horrobin
International Director of Ellel Ministries
Ellel Grange, Lancaster, England

Preface

In 1997, I prayed, "Lord, please disciple me." This book is both the story of how God discipled me and the biblical foundation of discipleship He taught me in answer to that prayer. I've experienced many answered prayers in my lifetime, and I've seen God do marvelous things. Yet this answer to prayer was significant enough that I knew God wanted me to write about it.

It's a miracle in itself that you would be reading anything I have written. If you could find my English teachers and tell them I wrote a book, you might discover that they remember me as perhaps the worst student they ever had! My handwriting looked—and still looks—a lot like hieroglyphics.

God could have chosen a much more eloquent or intelligent person—someone with far greater intellect and experience. Why He entrusted this message to me—a message I believe to be of paramount importance to every believer—I'll never even try to figure out. But in my own faltering way and to the best of my ability, I have tried to set before you what I believe Jesus intends for every believer. I also believe it's what every believer longs for in his or her heart. Most have given up finding it. Many have never allowed themselves to hope they could experience Jesus as His 12 disciples experienced Him.

The first half of this book chronicles my personal discipleship process. It tells the story of what God did in answer to my prayer, "Lord, disciple me!" Much of my early Christian life isn't worth writing about. I grew up in a wonderful Christian home, was called into ministry as a teenager, went to Bible college and seminary, and went into youth ministry with plans to pursue missions work. I read the same books everyone else read, went to the same conferences, and studied the same church-growth techniques.

I always loved reading the New Testament, and I wished I could have been with Jesus. I longed to see Him do miracles, heal the sick, cast out demons, and walk on water. I would have loved to hear Him teach. I often wished I could have been taught by Jesus all the things His disciples learned.

But it was as if since birth I'd been given a box—a "God Box," if you will. It wasn't an imaginary box, though no one could see it. The box was very real. The lid of this box was made up of all the beliefs I'd acquired through the years. Beliefs like:

- God doesn't do today what He did in the Bible.

- God doesn't use His people to heal the sick today.

- All the gifts of God are not for today.

- It's presumptuous to pray and expect God to give specific answers.

- Miracles like those in the Bible have ceased.

- People today don't have demons.

Perhaps these statements were not explicitly expressed in the church, but they were part of the "practical theology" I'd been taught and had embraced. Like the people Paul describes in Second Timothy 3:5—and like most believers I knew—I had a form of godliness but denied its power.

That's not to say we denied that God *had* power or that He'd done miracles. We didn't even deny that God *could* do miracles if He wanted to today. We simply didn't talk about these biblical realities in relation to our modern lives. I had never heard one message, read a single book, or attended a Sunday school class about healing, casting out evil spirits, or "the Kingdom of God."

Over the years, the box of what God could and could not do took shape. The sides were handed to me. Those sides formed the theological basis of why God didn't do today what He did throughout the Bible. I learned all kinds of things about why we don't see miracles today, why certain gifts ceased, *why* God doesn't speak directly to people any longer, why there are no visions and dreams, and why we don't do what the disciples did or what Jesus did.

I didn't want a box that limited God, but I accepted what my pastors and teachers taught me. I longed for an experience with God that was "outside the box," but I was faithful to hang onto my box—and even helped others with their boxes.

Then one day the most amazing thing happened. I got curious. I wanted to see what God looked like. I knew you weren't supposed to see God and live, but I couldn't stand it! So I peeled back the lid of my box and bent over to look inside.

I was shocked by what I saw. *Nothing!* There was nothing inside my box but cobwebs and dust. *What could this mean?* I wondered. But before I could consider it, *Kabooooom!* God exploded my box. Since that day, things have never been the same.

You may think I've made up or exaggerated some of what I've described in this book. Several times as I reread what I'd written, I found myself in tears as I stood in awe of God. What God did after He exploded my box is remarkable. I've seen and experienced more of God than I ever dreamed possible! Now He has led me to share it with you.

If you've been given a box that limits God in any way, I pray that you too will have your box exploded. It's scary, but don't worry. It gets worse!

It can be incredibly disconcerting to realize that your theology is messed up—especially for people like me who've been to Bible college and seminary and who go to every Bible study and seminar they can get to. When God begins to show you more of Himself, it can really rock your world.

Experiencing the God of the Bible is also the most rewarding and exciting journey imaginable. I wouldn't take a billion dollars for what you are about to read. I understand why the disciples could endure such persecution and keep telling the story. They didn't just have a theology. *They experienced God.*

There was no box to limit God or what He could do. I believe if the disciples saw the boxes we believe God fits in today, they'd weep. *I* sometimes weep as I look at the churches and the people filling the pews, adding reinforcements to their boxes. I long to run through those churches and explode their boxes as well.

I dare you! Look inside your box. Do you really think God can fit inside it?

CHAPTER 1

Close Encounters With God

Being on staff at a large and respected church at a relatively young age, I was very blessed. To be perfectly honest, I felt a sense of pride—but since pride doesn't sound quite as good, we'll stick with "blessed."

My title, director of student ministries, had a variety of meanings. It sounded more important than youth minister, but to many, it still meant "low man on the totem pole." Nevertheless, the student ministry of our church was growing and truly experiencing God's blessings. I had an awesome team of volunteer staff, whom I loved and who loved me as well as the students.

I remember walking the halls of our church and saying out loud, "I can't believe they pay me to do this!" There was a day when I couldn't have imagined working with teenagers, but now I couldn't imagine a more enjoyable group of people to serve. Teenagers were real. They were out to enjoy life, and they were radical. Every other ministry in the church looked boring compared to working with teenagers. The students saw it that way, and quite frankly, I agreed.

Everything about my life was going great. I had a beautiful wife, two lovely boys, and a ministry I loved doing every day.

Do you ever catch yourself in moments when everything seems to be going right? Each day is an adventure. You love what you do. You anticipate waking up every morning—and life seems to hold so much promise. Your hope is for everything to stay just the way it is. That's exactly where I was.

A Difficult Decision

There was only one catch. When God had called me into ministry, I'd committed to serve Him wherever He wanted our family to be, doing whatever He wanted us to do. For 15 years, I'd been certain that God wanted me in a foreign country where most of the people had never heard of Jesus. In the five years since completing my master's degree at Columbia International University, I had been serving at a huge church in sunny Florida, in a town that was filled with other big churches.

Surely God's plan couldn't include suntans, palm trees, and beaches! My wife, Dawn, and I were almost sure it was time to make a move. In fact, I was 99 percent certain God was directing me to a town just outside of Amsterdam, where I would be planting a new church. Soon I would close the door on this phase of ministry and begin the arduous process of support-raising and training. It was what I had studied and prepared for throughout seven years of college and seminary. After all, I had committed my life to missions at least ten times!

It was no secret to the church staff and our closest friends that our time at this church in Brandon was going to be short-term. We'd planned to spend a few years developing our skills and building a strong relationship with a local church before going overseas. Now was the moment of decision.

Those who knew about our plans to serve the Lord as missionaries seemed to be divided. Some were excited and encouraging. Then there were parents and close friends who loved us but thought we were crazy. Strangely, there were others whose opinions Dawn and I held in high regard, who told us in no uncertain terms that we were not going to go overseas!

One dear friend told us that God had shown her that we were not going to the mission field. She was sure of it! A close pastor friend shared with me his agreement. He felt that God still wanted to use us in Brandon. This was flattering and encouraging news, but it couldn't be God—could it?

At that point, I began to wonder. My background and training told me it would be foolish to remain in the United States, where there are an abundance of Christians and churches. I'd been in countries where fewer than half of 1 percent were evangelical Christians. On the other hand, my ministry was bearing fruit, and I still had a passion to reach out to the urban areas of Tampa and see God work in my city.

Dawn and I loved having so many Christian friends. I liked having a salary I could depend on. And I liked being on staff at a big church. *Surely,* I thought, *it's my flesh that's weak. It's tempting me to take the easy way out.* After all, wasn't it God's will for all Christians to die at the hand of some savage tribe while sharing the gospel? So Holland wasn't filled with savage tribes. With so few Christians there, I was sure we'd find plenty of ways to "suffer for Jesus!"

I was in an inner tug-of-war, and I needed to know God's will for my life. Both doorways stood before me, and both looked good. Either choice could have been God's will for Dawn and me.

I had always been taught that God doesn't have a specific will for His children—that either choice I made would be acceptable to Him. Let me clarify. What many believe and are taught is that God has given specific truths in the Bible. If we apply them to our lives, we will be in God's will. My teachers had impressed upon me that God doesn't speak to us directly with the details of what we're supposed to do. But now I was in a crisis of decision—torn between two great opportunities. That's when I decided to test the line of thinking I'd been taught.

Every believer who truly hungers for God's will comes to this point of decision. You can keep going in the direction you've been going, or you can change direction. For example, you can take a job that pays more money, or you can be a missionary. Both decisions may look good, and the answer isn't easy. These are the moments when we desperately want to hear God's audible voice. It is often in these major times of decision that we truly begin to seek the Lord.

Does your theology allow God to speak? If so, how does He speak? Is it only through His written Word? Does God still give His people visions and dreams? Does He still speak through prophets and angels? These were the things I needed to know.

Throughout the Bible, God spoke to His people in many varied ways. In the King James Version, the phrase similar to "saith the Lord" appears 815 times in the 66 books of the Bible, which is an average of 14 times per book. God appeared to Adam, Noah, Moses, Abraham, Isaac, Jacob, and Joshua—and He spoke to them. The prophets spoke what God told them to speak. God spoke in dreams, visions, and even directly to His people.

What many evangelicals teach today is that God only spoke to men and women occasionally throughout history. Now that we have the written Word, they say, God no longer speaks directly to His people.

A Unique Prayer

I thought I would be copping out if I chose to stay in Brandon rather than go overseas. So I committed to the harder road of following God's call to leave America and serve in Holland. At that point, I gave the Lord only two options for revealing His will if He wanted me to stay. If His perfect will included our staying in Florida, He could either drop a granite stone out of the sky, or He could send someone who didn't know me and whom I didn't know to tell me that God had told him that He wanted us to stay. We needed a supernatural answer.

Now, what made this prayer unusual is that the theological framework I'd been given didn't allow for God to speak so specifically or directly to people today. I'd been taught that since we have the written Word, God has pretty much told us what He has to say. If we follow God's Word, study, and pray, He'll show us His will through the Scriptures. According to my training, having determined to head out to the uttermost parts of the earth, I was already on track with God's will. I committed to fast for four days and make my primary focus to know God's will concerning our future. I told God all my thoughts and feelings. I told Him I wanted to go anywhere and do anything He wanted. As I prayed, my heart was more and more drawn toward the possibility of not going overseas. I had made the commitment that unless God showed me otherwise, I was gone—and I planned to stick with that commitment. As I finished the fast on Thursday, I knew there was only one way my course could be changed.

Gideon laid out a fleece before God in Judges 6:36-40. He did this two times and was specific in what he asked God to do so that there would be no doubting when He answered. One day Gideon wanted God to cause the fleece to be wet and the ground around the fleece to be dry. The next day the fleece was wet and the ground was dry. In fear and trembling, Gideon asked God to be patient with him. He wanted to obey but needed more assurance that he was following God's will. This time Gideon asked God to let the fleece be dry and the ground wet. God answered Gideon exactly the way he had asked.

Some say Gideon's prayer was immature and that God doesn't answer prayers like that today. Some would teach Gideon's actions were not ideal acts of faith; he had already heard God's will from God Himself. Clearly, the time of Judges was a downward spiral in Israel's history, and from other passages about Gideon, it seems that he wasn't necessarily dwelling in God's perfect will (see Judg. 8:24-27).

It's in times like that—when you feel that a decision is critical to your future and God's purposes—the still, small voice of God becomes difficult to discern. You begin asking yourself, "Is that God or my own feelings?"

I now realize that a "fleece" doesn't threaten God. God responds when His children are diligently longing to hear His voice and obey. I needed to know God's plan, so I laid out my fleece and set a course that I believed was His will. I wanted to give God a clear way to show me that He had a different plan for me. It's also important that I fasted while seeking God. There's something about fasting that clears away any self-will and opens communication between us and God.

Daniel fasted in Daniel 9 and again in Daniel 10 when he was seeking God for answers. In each case, God sent an angel to deliver a message to Daniel. In both instances, the angel said that an answer had been sent as soon as Daniel had begun praying. One time we're told the answer took 21 days to arrive. (Sounds like snail mail, doesn't it?) The reality, we're told in Daniel, was that there was a spiritual battle going on in the heavens.

Though I'd been "taught better," I laid out a fleece and set my face to pray and fast for God's answer. When was the last time you became that desperate in seeking God? There is nothing as exciting as a holy desperation for God!

God's Surprising Answer

On the Monday after my four-day fast, we'd wrapped up a staff meeting and I was back at my desk. The rest of the staff had gone to lunch, so I was the only pastor in the office. Shirley, our receptionist, buzzed my phone and asked if I'd be available to talk to someone who wanted to speak to a pastor. I put down what I was working on and made my way to the reception area to greet this person in need.

amazon.co.uk

Thank you for shopping at Amazon.co.uk!

A2

Invoice for
Your order of 7 November, 2013
Order ID 026-3642181-8071557
Invoice number D.VwMsB9N
Invoice date 20 November, 2013

Billing Address
Mr R Rudge
Swainston Lodge
Calbourne
Newport, Isle of Wight po30 4hx
United Kingdom

Shipping Address
Mr R Rudge
Swainston Lodge
Calbourne
Newport, Isle of Wight po30 4hx
United Kingdom

Qty.	Item	Our Price (excl. VAT)	VAT Rate	Total Price
1	**The Jesus Training Manual** Paperback, Richard Mull. 0768437466 (** p-4 E21B92 **)	£9.99	0%	£9.99
	Shipping charges	£0.00		£0.00
	Subtotal (excl. VAT) 0%			£9.99
	Total VAT			£0.00
	Total			£9.99

Conversion rate · £1.00 : EUR 1.19

This shipment completes your order.

You can always check the status of your orders or change your account details from the Your Account link at the top of each page on our site.

Thinking of returning an item? PLEASE USE OUR ON-LINE RETURNS SUPPORT CENTRE.

Our Returns Support Centre (www.amazon.co.uk/returns-support) will guide you through our Returns Policy and provide you with a printable, personalised return label. Please have your order number ready (you can find it next to your order summary, above). Our Returns Policy does not affect your statutory rights.

Amazon EU S.à r.l., 5 Rue Plaetis, L-2338, Luxembourg
VAT number : GB727255821

Please note - this is not a returns address - for returns - please see above for details of our online returns centre

0/DpVNMDB4N/-1 of 1-//SMDA/econ-uk/10126405/1123 15:00/1121 00:41 Pack Type : A2

At first glance, I knew this encounter would be interesting. Before me was an older man with long hair pulled back in a ponytail and a long beard. Half his teeth were missing, and his hands were very dirty. Outside the door behind him, I could see the most dented, dirty, old pickup I'd ever seen outside a salvage yard. The truck had a long, flatbed trailer filled with all kinds of scrap metal. I had not a clue what was about to unfold.

The man introduced himself as Pastor Cecil and proceeded to explain his appearance. The reason he looked the way he did was that he ministered to the homeless, to prostitutes, and to homosexuals and transvestites in the inner city of Tampa. He said the people he ministered to wouldn't listen to someone like me. I figured he had a point there. So what did this guy want?

He told me that God had sent him to our office to speak to a pastor. I was sure he was going to ask for some money for his ministry, but instead he said, "The only thing I know I'm supposed to say is this: Sometimes we feel that the only place God can use us is in another country or far away, when in reality, God wants us to stay right where we are—and right where we are is where God can use us to make an impact." The man began to weep and tremble as he continued, "I don't know why I'm saying this, but God told me to come in here today and tell this to a pastor."

I almost fell to the floor right then and there. God had heard my prayer! He cared about my life and had sent the most unlikely messenger to deliver the answer.

I invited the man back to my office, where he proceeded to give me Ezekiel 2, 3, and 33. He told me that these passages related specifically to my calling. He gave me several other passages and answered two other very specific prayers I had prayed that week. Pastor Cecil told me that I was to stay away from all intoxicants and that God was going to use me in the inner city of Tampa. That week I had been praying about God's will for me concerning wine and beer, since all the missionaries I knew in Europe drank in social settings. I had also asked God why I had such a burden for the inner city of Tampa, when I was living in suburbia and heading overseas.

My new friend concluded our brief meeting with a song and a kiss on the cheek. How else do you top off an encounter like that? Right about now, a little song and a kiss didn't seem so strange in the context of everything that had transpired in just 15 minutes.

I just stood there in a daze. I was shocked on the one hand, yet somewhere deep inside I had expected God to do something unique in answer to my prayer.

When the shock wore off, I called Dawn and told her what had happened. She was just as stunned and excited as I was, and she couldn't wait to hear more. I told her I'd be coming home early. How could I get back to working after what had just happened? Then I went out to the receptionist, to make sure she'd heard the same things I had. Shirley had known about what I'd been praying and said, "Was that what I thought it was? Did that guy just tell you you're supposed to stay here?" I thought, *Great! So I wasn't dreaming. This really did happen.*

I could never have known how unsettling it would be to have such a specific prayer answered in such an unusual way. The good thing was, now I didn't have to wonder about where I was supposed to live. I didn't have to question whether I had taken the easy way out. I didn't have to worry that I'd somehow missed God's ultimate will.

Though the church had begun looking for my replacement, they immediately accepted me back into the role I'd been serving in for several years. I called our friends and told them about God's answer to our prayer. They rejoiced, and everyone knew God's hand had moved in a special way.

What would you do if God answered your prayer in such a unique way? Have you ever experienced such a dramatic response to a specific request? If you've been taught that God doesn't work in the same way today as He did long ago, what would you do with an encounter like that?

Throughout the Bible, God spoke through unusual people who listened and heard His voice. To Abraham, God sent Melchizedek, who spoke a blessing to him before God gave Abraham a vision. To Joshua, God sent "the commander of the Lord's army," who told Joshua how to take the city (see Josh. 5:15). In Joshua's case, we're told that the messenger was the Lord. Some scholars believe that this was a pre-incarnate appearance of Jesus Himself. The Bible doesn't specifically tell us who this person was, except that He was called the Lord (see Josh. 5:13–6:7). So it seems that God Himself showed up in human form to speak to Joshua.

God often sent prophets to His servants throughout the Word. We see Samuel speaking God's message to Saul and David. We see Nathan speaking God's message to David. God gave supernatural knowledge to men and women throughout the Scriptures. Abraham was called a prophet by God when he encountered Abimelech. So why does it surprise so many of us that God would use someone to bring a clear answer to prayer today?

It's critical for us to know that God can and does do the supernatural and the miraculous today. God wants us to ask great things of Him. Remember that my prayer was in the context of serving Jesus with my whole life and my whole future.

If we ask God for the supernatural so that we can get something or experience something cool, then God is not obliged to act. In fact, that's why so many who have prayed for God to do something supernatural have wound up disappointed.

God knows our own hearts better than we do. If we are testing Him or would become prideful when He answers, then God waits until we are fully surrendered to Him.

It's also important to understand that God loves holy desperation. He longs for us to stop running our own show and seek Him with prayer and fasting. Many times we're like children who want to do a project all by ourselves. We get out the glue and scissors, some paper and some sticks, and start trying to build a model. We say, "I can do it, Daddy! Watch me!" Then we get frustrated. What we wanted to make is not what's happening. The whole project begins to look like a mess. Some children, out of frustration, look at Dad and blame him. Others look at the mess and bring it to Dad to work on.

Now is the time to stop running ahead with all your plans. It's time instead to give them all to God. Are you willing to lay down your future? Are you willing to lay down your theology if God wants to rewrite it? God beats any theologian known to man! His Word is perfect. His will is perfect. We have to begin to pray, saying, "Whatever You want, God, I will do. I'll go where You want me to go, do what You want me to do, and say what You want me to say." When we pray like that, God can pick up the pieces of our mess and begin making something more exciting and more powerful than we could ever make.

Unsettling Questions

A myriad of questions began to fill my mind. How did this guy know what I had prayed and what God wanted to tell me? Could someone have told him about my prayer? I had told only a handful of close friends about the direction we were headed. Even fewer knew about my specific prayer. Could this man have been the devil's messenger? I knew that the devil has less power than God and that his knowledge and territory are limited. I couldn't imagine God allowing satan to answer my prayer! Could this be one of the greatest coincidences of all time?

I came to a conclusion, and the answer was obvious. God had a specific plan for my future. He cared about me and had listened to my prayers. He was intimately involved in the details of my life.

God had broken into my very natural existence in a supernatural way. Pastors and teachers had taught me that God doesn't speak directly to His people anymore. It was obvious that the man God used to speak to me didn't believe that at all. God had spoken to Pastor Cecil, and he had listened to God at the risk of being ridiculed and called crazy.

Now I wondered, *Could God speak to me like He spoke to Cecil?* I knew that if God wanted something specific told to someone, He couldn't count on me. I didn't know how to hear His voice. Then Jesus' words in John 10:3-5, 16, and 27 came to my mind. Each of these verses speaks of God's voice—and of His sheep knowing His voice and following it. I was broken. God had nailed me. I had denied His voice nearly all of my life. I knew in an instant that I had heard the voice of God many times, but my rational mind always debated it and rationalized away what God was saying. Could that truly be God speaking to me? Isn't it really just my mind? Could it be the devil?

What I had been taught about how God speaks was not wrong. It was just incomplete. I had been taught that if you stick with the written Word, you can't go wrong. How true that is—but it's only part of the truth.

Now, day after day, I began to fall on the floor, asking God to teach me to hear His voice. I wanted to know the Shepherd's voice. I wanted God to be able to use me. If the Shepherd still spoke to His sheep directly about details, not contradicting His written Word, then I wanted to know how to listen. I wanted to hear God's voice on issues not explicitly covered in Scripture.

For example, how would God answer the question, "Lord, do You want me to serve You as a pastor or as a businessperson?" Both a pastor and a businessperson can be instrumental in building God's Kingdom. You might think that being a pastor is more "spiritual" and that God would undoubtedly desire that for your life. Or you might rationalize that God wants people to be in business and make a lot of money to support the work of His ministry. Both are great ambitions, but which is God's will for you? What if God needs you to learn something through business so that you can be a better pastor than you would have been? What if God knows that He's given you the special ability to build a business that could financially support 500 pastors with twice your ability?

God's perspective is not only better than ours; it's perfect! That's why we need to hear His voice. If we don't hear from God and get His direction for our lives, we'll miss the greatest that God has for us. In short, if you don't ask God to teach you how to hear His voice, then you'll never hear it.

The Word of God is filled with stories of God speaking to people. From Genesis to Revelation, God was in the business of speaking to His own. God even spoke to heathen people. He used visions and dreams and spoke directly to more people than I could count. I realized that not only was it possible for God to speak to me, but I was also pretty certain He'd been speaking to me all my life! I just hadn't learned to listen to His voice and His will.

For more biblical discipleship go to: www.operationlightforce.com.

Study Questions

1. Have you faced a difficult decision where both options looked good but they would lead you down very different paths? Write or tell about one of these decisions you faced. How did you decide?

   _____

   _____

   _____

2. Write and/or tell about a situation you faced where you really needed to know God's will.

   _____

   _____

3. Read Judges 6:36-39. How does Gideon ask the Lord to confirm what God's will is in regard to fighting against the enemy? Does the Bible teach that we should do this whenever we ask for His will?

_____

_____

_____

4. Read Daniel 9:3,20-23, and Daniel 10:2-14. When Daniel needed to know God's will, what was his pattern? How did God respond to this? (Notice what the angel says in verses 9:23, 10:11, and 10:19.)

_____

_____

_____

5. Have you ever heard the Lord's voice? Describe it.

_____

_____

_____

6. What decision have you faced recently where it would be critical to know what God's will is for your life? What is the surest way to find God's will about any subject?

_____

_____

_____

CHAPTER 2

God Explodes My Box

So what do you do when God has turned your world upside down? When everything you believed about God is brought into question and you realize that He's so much bigger and greater than anything you could ever have imagined? None of what transpired with Cecil fit either my theology of what God does or my personal experience of what God is like. What if someone showed up at your office with a specific message from God that fit every detail of your prayer? How would you respond?

You'd have several choices. You could choose to ignore it. You could plug your ears and say, "I don't want to hear anything that doesn't fit into my neat little compartments of what the world is supposed to be like." Or you could begin to respond and ask God to teach you more.

We have to admit that all of us have a sort of "God box." We may say that God can do anything, but our practical belief system would limit much of what we believe God actually does today.

It is important to pursue God with a mixture of caution and abandon. On the one hand, you have to understand that there are many in the Body of Christ who are wolves in sheep's clothing. It is a fact that false doctrines have arisen and people have built theologies that are in complete contradiction of Scripture. It's equally true that God has so much more for us than our miniature views of Him have allowed. God wants to destroy the boxes or limitations that exist only in our minds and experience and prove Himself to be so much greater. God is longing for us to begin pursuing Him in all of His glory and power.

The way to pursue God with caution and abandon is to spend time in His Word and in prayer. This is what the Bereans did in Acts 17:11:

> *Now the Bereans were of more noble character than the Thessalonians, for they received the message with great eagerness and examined the Scriptures every day to see if what Paul said was true.*

I always believed that Paul was simply teaching doctrine, but we know that Paul walked in an amazing demonstration of God's power. A significant amount of what Paul taught would have been based on His daily walk with God. In Acts 19, we see Paul doing extraordinary miracles. How could we not see his teaching in the light of what he did in ministry? Most of my Christian life was like that. If Paul was teaching that he had special abilities and a unique experience with God that no one else could attain, then he would have stated that. Instead, he defended his teaching by pointing to the reality of God's power at work in his life. First Corinthians 2:4 states, *"My message and my preaching were not with wise and persuasive words, but with a demonstration of the Spirit's power."*

When we examine everything in the light of God's Word and then ask God to bring His Word to life within us, exciting things begin to happen. Most people study to fill their minds with God's Word. We need to begin to passionately pursue God's Word in a new way. We must cry out for God to bring His Word to life within us. God wants His Word to be living in us. We need to begin to act upon what we know, and God's Word will become alive to us in ways we never dreamed possible.

I recently heard someone preaching on the resurrection. He was using material that I had used before and others had used with details about what Jesus experienced. The words were lifeless and dead. The preacher had a great personality and could formulate words well. He was great looking, but the message was devoid of life and power. His experience with God seemed mostly cognitive.

Most of my experience with God up until now in the story had been cognitive—based on filling my brain with truths and concepts. Now I was beginning to live what I had always read, believed, and sought to understand, and the Word of God became alive! When I talk about living out what the Word of God says, I'm not talking about going to church, teaching a Sunday school class, or doing some good deed. We need to begin to experience God's Word at a deeper level. We need to join God in doing what His Word says we can do.

I chose to passionately pursue God and listen to His voice with that mixture of caution and abandon. I would examine everything from God's Word that I was experiencing and at the same time allow God's Word to be the standard rather than my theology or past experiences.

One way I began to pursue God was by responding to His call on my life. I now began to invest my energies in mobilizing students to reach out to the inner city. The longing in my heart to reach outside our nice, suburban community and fulfill God's Word to care for the poor, the fatherless, and the widows led me to some new adventures.

At a Promise Keepers rally, I had committed to develop a relationship with someone of another race. Now I was seeking to mobilize the youth of our church to do so as well. God opened the door for me to be able to develop a close relationship with an African American pastor named Jeff. A close friend who knew of my desire had heard of Jeff and his desire for the same type of relationship. For our first meeting, Jeff and I met at a restaurant for breakfast. We had hardly introduced ourselves when Jeff said, "God wants us to plant a church together." Well, that's not what I had in mind, nor was it what I had expected from this visit! I told Jeff that God was going to have to show me if it was His will for us to plant a church, but that I was ready to build a relationship and bring our youth to his inner-city church to help do outreaches.

After that breakfast, Jeff and I began to meet once a week. All my years of missionary training caused me to immerse myself in seeking to understand the African American culture. Here we were, living in the same town, only miles apart, yet I had never before invested the emotional energy to build a serious relationship with an African American.

Jeff was a patient teacher. I asked him questions about everything. Why do you do church like this? How do you feel about that? What can I do to make right some wrong that has been done? Even deeply personal questions about differences in the ways we thought, the foods we ate, and the ways we talked were fair game with Jeff.

In small ways, over the next few years, I would be forever changed. For the first time in my life, the barriers that separated me from my African American brothers were coming down. I realized from God's Word that the barriers had already been destroyed through Christ's blood, and that the separation that existed between us was a result of sin.

For He Himself is our peace, who has made the two one and has destroyed the barrier, the dividing wall of hostility (Ephesians 2:14).

I also began to grapple with the fact that my forefathers were the perpetrators of many cruel and inhumane injustices, although I cannot point to an act of any specific relative. I was made strongly aware of the fact that my people—the generations that preceded me—had raped, murdered, bought, sold, abused, and degraded a whole race of people for whom Christ had died.

This was not the kind of thing that was spoken of in our home growing up. It wasn't what my relatives chose to talk about. I honestly don't know anything about how my ancestors treated the slaves they may have owned. I had never even taken the time to think about whether my forefathers had owned any slaves. It was as if nothing like that had ever happened. But that cannot be said of the victims of those gross sins. In many African American homes, the grandparents or great-grandparents experienced these atrocities. The Lord began to show me what I could do to heal the hurt, in some small way, and to break the curse that was brought on my people through our sin. Jesus had paid the price to atone the debt that I owed my brothers. I couldn't pay for the sins of my forefathers. Jesus already had paid it. I could appropriate that payment by asking God's forgiveness, and I could be an agent of God's healing in the hearts of those whose forefathers had been the victims.

God's Word clearly teaches us that sin has an effect on more than just those who do the sin. We can bring a curse on our children for three or four generations. In Numbers 14:18, we read:

The Lord is slow to anger, abounding in love and forgiving sin and rebellion. Yet He does not leave the guilty unpunished; He punishes the children for the sin of the fathers to the third and fourth generation.

Deuteronomy 5:9 says,

You shall not bow down to them or worship them; for I, the Lord your God, am a jealous God, punishing the children for the sin of the fathers to the third and fourth generation of those who hate Me.

(Also see Exodus 20:5 and 34:7.)

The exciting news, however, is that God's Word also promises that His blessings are passed on to a thousand generations. Deuteronomy 5:10 says that God shows *"love to a thousand generations of those who love Me and keep My commandments."* The sins and faithfulness of my forefathers have indeed brought both curses and blessings.

Let me clarify that in my family, there have been many more blessings passed on than curses. As I researched my family background, most of what I found was encouraging. There were senators and school superintendents, preachers, and other men of honor. Nevertheless, I was struck with the reality that there were barriers I needed to destroy and curses I needed God to break—that is, if I was going to be effective at ministering in this new arena.

As God opened doors in church after church, He led me repeatedly to begin my message with public repentance to my African American brothers for the sins of my forefathers and for my own sin of indifference and willful ignorance. In each case, God then did a healing work. Some of the healing was in my own life over issues I hadn't even known existed. Proverbs 14:34 (NKJV) tells us, *"Righteousness exalts a nation, but sin is a reproach to any people."* The sins of my forefathers had brought a reproach on my people.

As God led me to repent for the sins of my forefathers, it was more than rhetoric. I knew that He had called me to minister reconciliation and that this would also heal me of any curse that had been brought on me by the sins of my forefathers. This was one facet of God's calling that took me way outside my comfort zone. Yet it was in total obedience to Him. This act of obedience led to many incredibly exciting experiences with God. It also brought healing to me that I had no idea I even needed.

Within six months of my dramatic encounter with Cecil, God had convinced me that it truly was His will for me to leave my nice, comfortable, suburban church and to immerse myself in the inner city of Tampa. God had used Jeff's constant, gentle, and even not-so-gentle reminders that we were going to plant a church. God had also used major upheavals at the church where I still ministered—as well as the still, small voice that I was learning to hear—to confirm that I was following Him.

I had been studying *Experiencing God* by Henry T. Blackaby and Claude V. King and had come to the conclusion that I wasn't interested in just a little bit of God. I wanted everything God had for me! There was no holding back. I wanted to lay it all out for God and experience Him in ways you read about in the Bible but don't often see today.

Nearly every roller coaster has a caution sign before you board the ride. There's usually an extensive list of warnings and conditions that must be met if you want to experience the ride, and it's often enough to scare many potential riders away! For others, the warning only adds to the excitement and anticipation of the thrill ahead.

At this point, I want to issue a caution.

If you decide to do more than just read a book like *Experiencing God* and truly live what God's Word says, it will mess up your neat little religion. In a later chapter, we will examine Paul's experience in greater detail, but let me point out something here: After Paul's dramatic encounter with Christ on the road to Damascus, his nice little religion was destroyed. His whole purpose in life took a 180-degree turn. His theology was radically altered in a matter of minutes. It's exciting to experience God and get outside of our "God box." But it's also very scary.

Touched by God's Power

As I was beginning to pursue God, one day I got a phone call. It was Cecil again. After our first brief encounter, I had wondered if God had sent an angel. In fact, for some time, I was convinced that Cecil must have been an angel and not a real person. He wasn't what I'd envisioned an angel looking like, but who was I to judge? Cecil told me that God had given him another word for me. Well, I was all ears! I knew that God had spoken to this man once, and it had changed my life. Still, I was apprehensive, and many questions and doubts still rolled around in my head. What would happen this time? Should I run from this meeting or run to it?

Everyone I knew had heard about Cecil and our first encounter. Most people wanted to see him. When he arrived at the church, we headed back to my office. Along the way, secretaries and staff members stepped into the hallway, and Cecil began to minister to them. Again, I was in awe as he spoke to them of deeply personal things that no one could have known about their lives. I had never told Cecil anything about anyone in the office. He'd pray over them and maybe sing them a song. One lady fell to the floor, and I was certain this was going to be my last day on the job. I figured word would spread that I had brought in this weird guy who was doing some strange things that our church didn't believe in.

When we got to my office, Cecil said, "Before I share the words God has given me for you, we need to go to your home and pray for your wife. She's having severe back pain and needs prayer." Again, I was shocked! How did this guy know these things? Sure enough, Dawn was three months pregnant with our third child and was having problems with her sciatic nerve. The very night before, she had cried out in pain during the middle of the night.

So Jeff, Cecil, and I got into our cars and headed to my house. Jeff never shied away from adventure, and he had come because he wanted to see the guy God had used to get me out of my comfort zone.

When we got to my home, Cecil prayed over Dawn, anointed her with oil, read some Scripture, and Dawn was healed. Her back pains instantly ceased! When he turned to give me the word God had spoken to him for me, I was ready. I don't remember what he said, but when Cecil began to pray, something happened. I felt a surge of power and collapsed to the floor.

Exactly one week before, I had been speaking with a student about how all this falling out, "slain in the Spirit" stuff was not of God. Seeking to straighten him out, I had asked this student to show me a verse in the Bible about being slain in the Spirit. For me to be lying on the carpet one week later was the last thing I would ever have expected. As I lay there with my eyes closed, I saw a vision of a man standing at my feet (another new experience that didn't fit my paradigm). At first, I was certain that the man I saw was an angel; then I thought he was just a man. This man began to drape a cloth over my body. I wasn't conscious of anyone around me until I heard Cecil say, "There is an angel who is placing a mantle on you." I was intent on what I was experiencing, but I also wondered, "How could this guy know what I'm seeing?"

For about ten minutes, I was unable to move. I saw pictures and moving images more real than any dream or movie I had ever seen. The visions had a vivid, three-dimensional brilliance unlike anything I'd ever witnessed before. I watched a sword fall from the sky and split a veil that separated me from another realm. Then I saw a little angel with the most joyful expression invite me to come behind the veil. Behind the veil, I saw a Roman soldier's helmet floating over a small platform. At this point, Dawn stooped down to make sure I was still breathing.

If my last encounter with Cecil hadn't messed me up, this one surely had to. I didn't believe in any of the things that were going on, but they were going on and they were happening to me. I imagine I was feeling something similar to what scientists who believed man would never fly must have felt when the Wright brothers first flew at Kitty Hawk. Sure, the Bible was full of healings. But they didn't happen like that in any of the churches I'd attended or in any of my educational training. And yeah, God gave visions to many people throughout the Bible. But nobody I'd ever known had visions. And this "slain in the Spirit" stuff—wasn't that all fake? You couldn't show it to me in the Bible, could you? I'd heard that the ministry of Charles Finney was the greatest of all time, and that people "fell out" many times during his meetings. And in the Bible, people always fell when God's glory showed up, but not today. This was not how God worked. It didn't fit my "God box."

Critical Analysis

What would you think at this point? How would you be feeling? My head was spinning. This was pushing my theological envelope to the breaking point. It was also the most incredible thing I had ever experienced! Either I was experiencing the supernatural God of the Bible and the things my heroes of the faith had written about, or something else was going on. I was deeply analytical in my thinking, but each time I analyzed, the conclusion was the same. God was touching my world. He was rocking my very foundations.

The response was immediate. I wanted to know God more than ever. I wanted to know the God of Abraham, Isaac, and Jacob. I wanted everything He had for me—nothing more, nothing less! I had seen an angel, felt the fire of God, seen my wife healed, had a man sent from God deliver a word in answer to my prayer—and I was forever changed.

You cannot read what I've shared and not react in some way. Perhaps you're beginning to sense something stirring inside. There's an anticipation…an excitement. Is it really possible to experience God in such personal, dramatic, and supernatural ways? In your heart, you have longed to see God do the things you've read about in Scripture.

Others may be thinking that I've fabricated this entire story. You've never heard of God doing the things I've described. You want to put the book away and write me off. Or perhaps you're searching for a rational explanation for what I have shared. You think, *Maybe the Florida sun was baking his brains, or he must be suffering from delusions of grandeur.*

Do you long for God to break in and touch your world? To many, God seems to be distant. To others, He seems very close. Perhaps when you pray, you know God is there. You don't have any particular desire for more. You're content with where you are spiritually. But God wants to be even more real in your life. He wants to take you past a devotional experience. He wants you to know Him in His power. God wants you to know Him in ways you've never dreamed possible. Be open to all that He has for you.

My First Extended Fast

It was nearly Christmas. I was leaving my large, suburban church to plant a new church in the inner city. I was stepping out in faith, and God was beginning to work in ways I never could have dreamed. I was hungrier for God than ever before.

As I sought to hear His voice, I believed God was calling me to fast from Christmas to New Year's. I would get up around five in the morning and head to the church, where I would pray, read God's Word, and play my guitar from six until noon. I wanted to spend the first week of my new ministry being with God. During that week of fasting, Jeff became impressed that God was leading the church to fast for the first week of the New Year, so I committed to continue for that week as well. Now, you've got to realize that for someone who's known as "Sticks," who has never done more than a three-day fast, this was pretty scary.

Every morning, I'd get up and head to our new church in inner-city Tampa. I would sit at the altar and seek God in His Word and in prayer. It was a new year, and I was making a transition. I wanted to start it off right. Different friends came by and joined me for an hour here or there. Every minute of those two weeks, it seemed like God was speaking to me louder and clearer than ever before. The Word came alive and became so much simpler. God began to teach me things I had never heard before about how He made disciples and how we were to make disciples. I began to see more clearly that I had held God in a box—and that in reality, God was so much bigger than my box.

On New Year's Eve, our church had a "Watch Night" service, which is a tradition in many African American churches. Knowing nothing about the service, I looked forward to it. It was traditional that each of the church's male leadership (elders, deacons, and other spiritual men) would take turns preaching for ten minutes. There were about ten men selected, and I was asked to share as well. I was bringing up the rear, so I figured everyone would be half asleep by the time I spoke—or looking at their watches, wondering if it was time to leave. As a result, I planned a simple, short devotional.

Little did I know that a "Watch Night" service is really a preaching competition! Picture this: Here I was, from my seeker-sensitive, contemporary, casual, laid-back, suburban Florida church, jumping into a preaching competition with—get this—black preachers! Funny? Scary? Take your pick!

As I sat there that night, fear came over me. If you're an athlete, you know the kind of fear I'm talking about. This was that motivational fear that a batter feels when he's facing the best pitcher in the league. It's the kind you feel when your opponent is expected to take your little body and mop off the field with it. I wanted the Rapture to come right then and there! This was my first responsibility at the new church, and I didn't want to fail.

There was the pastor's son, who was 16 but preached like a seasoned veteran. There was the used car salesman, who knew he had one sermon each year and had taken all year to craft his ten-minute message. There were eight other men who had salivated over this moment since last New Year's Eve. And then there was me! I hadn't spent an hour on my ten-minute devotional. I knew I was toast. So I prayed hard—the kind of prayer a teenager prays at exam time, the kind of prayer many pray around April 15 every year. I'd been talking with God all week! Why hadn't He warned me about this?

As soon as I prayed, the peace of God filled my soul. Then the Lord told me that what I had prepared wasn't what He wanted me to say, and the peace left just as quickly as it had come! What? It usually takes me at least 15 hours of study to be ready to preach. Then the Lord told me He would give me the words to say.

The "Exploding Boxes" Sermon

I stood up and began to describe the box that had been given to me. I told of the theological "truths" I'd been taught about God and how He operates. I told them how I had learned that God doesn't speak directly to His people today, but only through the written Word. This was one side of my box.

I also told them I had been taught that many of the gifts were not for today—how God had ceased healing the sick and casting out evil spirits. And the sides of my box began to take shape.

I spoke of the different limitations our modern God was forced to fit into, and how these made our Christianity so different from that of the Gospels or Acts. I told them how I'd learned that because of modern psychology and medicine, healing and deliverance weren't necessary anymore.

There I stood before the congregation, feeling vulnerable. As I constructed this invisible box before their eyes, the truth was hitting me. God wasn't in my box. Right in front of them, I peeled back a corner of my imaginary little box, and sadly declared as I peered inside, "God is not here." I stood there in silence for a minute, and then said, as loud as I could, "In this new year, 1997, God is going to *boom!*" Everyone jumped. "God is going to explode our boxes and show us that He is soooo much greater than we can comprehend!"

I told how God had begun to destroy my box and show Himself to me. I spoke of what I believed God was going to do, and the entire congregation rose to their feet and cheered wildly. I knew that in the hearts of all believers was the desire to experience God in greater ways. Nearly every believer who studies God's Word wishes he or she could have been there when Jesus walked on water, made the blind see, caused the lame to walk, or set captives free. Studying and reading about what God did is more exciting than any novel. But living it firsthand? Nothing can compare!

I knew I hadn't won the competition that night, since it wasn't a competition anyway. God had ruled the night. God would rule the year. The congregation left with an electric anticipation of what the year ahead held in store.

When I left the church at 3:00 A.M. and found my van broken into and running, I had a few moments of doubt. In the back of my van were thousands of dollars worth of things to be given away. They were untouched.

The lock had been taken off and the ignition panel broken so that the van could be hot-wired. But the van was still sitting there. Why had the robbers left it? I knew then that angels were watching out for me.

The week before I left Calvary Church, one of the pastors, Earl Smith, had a dream. In his dream, I was in the inner city, in one of the worst sections of town. Earl said that he remembered feeling afraid for me. He remembered one time when he'd driven through that area and someone had just been shot. In the dream, he heard a voice. It was God's voice telling him that he didn't need to worry about me. Another woman from the staff had a similar dream. Again, God was showing me clearly that He could touch my world in supernatural ways. No one in my life had ever had a dream for me. This was getting exciting.

Things at the new church, called Mission of Love, went well. In six months, we grew rapidly, and the offerings nearly doubled. Still, for reasons unknown to me, God chose to end that phase of ministry for us after only a short time. But God uses the seeming tragedies in our lives to shape us, mold us, and build in us Christlike character. On the day my third child, Rachel, was born, my responsibilities at the new church ceased. I could only wonder what the next chapter would hold in this adventure of God's Word coming to life.

Study Questions

1. Have you ever experienced a time when God seemed to turn your whole world upside down and you came to question everything you had been taught? Describe what that was like.

2. How would you respond to someone showing up at your home or office with a very specific answer to something you prayed? Would you be skeptical?

_____

_____

_____

_____

3. Read Acts 17:11. What does this verse teach us as a method for finding out God's truth and His will?

_____

_____

_____

_____

4. Is there a difference between filling our minds with God's Word and living/experiencing God's Word?

_____

_____

_____

_____

5. Did this chapter make you feel uncomfortable, excited, angry, or something else? Why?

_____

_____

_____

6. What are facets of the "God boxes" that you received growing up?
   (These are things you were taught to be true that limit who God is and
   what God can do.)

_____

_____

_____

CHAPTER 3

Hearing God's Voice

For the next three months, Dawn and I wrestled with the idea of listening to God's voice. We had been taught that when the Scriptures were canonized—assembled into what is now known as the Bible—everything God had to say was to be found in the Bible. Like most everyone we knew, we believed that God doesn't give special revelation today outside of His Word. Of course, God could use circumstances, good preaching, and wise counsel—but not direct revelation of specific details. Things like what happened when Cecil showed up—or hearing a still, small voice saying, "Trust me for your finances and I will teach you My ways"—were strictly for loonies!

The question then presented itself: "How could Cecil have known what I was praying for?" The first possibility was that by sheer coincidence this man had walked into our church, asked for a pastor, met me (the only one out of ten pastors who was in the office at the time), and said some things that precisely answered my prayers. Another possibility, some suggested, was that Cecil was a psychic (or worse) and had tapped into some demonic source of information.

The only other plausible possibility I could think of was that God had spoken directly to him, revealed the specific answer to my prayer, told him where to go and when to tell it, and led him to the right person. The answer to my question may seem obvious to you, but it depends on your perspective. If God doesn't speak directly today apart from Scripture, then one of the first two possibilities (coincidence or that Cecil was a psychic) would be the obvious choice.

There was a serious problem with believing Cecil's message came from satan. If satan was the entity involved in answering my prayer, then he is more powerful and personal than God. Would God have allowed him to know and answer prayers I had shared with only a few close friends? Would God remain silent and let satan answer the sincere prayers of one of His servants?

To me, the possibility that all of this was a coincidence was as plausible as revolution. I'm no mathematician, but I'd venture that the odds of someone praying a prayer as specific as mine and someone who'd never met me answering that prayer are less likely than my winning the lottery without ever buying a ticket! In 34 years of life, no one had ever spoken to me or anyone I knew as Cecil had. I'd never prayed for anything remotely like what I'd asked for that week. The details of Cecil's answer were too specific and answered precisely what I had asked God for in prayer. The mathematical probability of this encounter being a coincidence seemed absurd.

Most would have to agree that God had broken through time and space and had proven that He speaks in detail today. God picked one of the few people who was crazy enough to obey a request like the one I'd made. No one I had ever known spent time listening to God. God spoke to Cecil, told him to walk into our building and ask for a pastor—trusting it would be the right one—and deliver the Word of the Lord at my specific request.

Can I Hear God, Too?

If God had to deliver a specific message to someone, would you be someone He would choose? Have you learned to hear God's voice? Would you be willing to act on that still, small voice, having the confidence and courage to go up to a total stranger and put your reputation on the line?

We have to wrestle with the question, "Does God still speak today?" And if He does speak today, the issue becomes, "Can I hear His voice?" John 10:3-5 clearly teaches that God speaks and we must learn to hear His voice:

The watchman opens the gate for him, and the sheep listen to his voice. He calls his own sheep by name and leads them out. When he has brought out all his own, he goes on ahead of them, and his sheep follow him because they know his voice. But they will never follow a stranger; in fact, they will run away from him because they do not recognize a stranger's voice.

Jesus taught His disciples that it is critical for His sheep to hear His voice and discern the difference between the voice of God and all other voices that seek to distract us.

The next question I grappled with was, "Can I hear God as well?" I knew that if someone else prayed a prayer like mine, God couldn't use me (or anyone else I could think of) to answer it. Normal people just don't hear God like that! And normal Christians don't go traipsing up to people they don't know and give them a message from God.

Yet since I wanted to experience God and had decided to go the distance with Him, I wanted to know God in this way. I wanted Him to be able to use me this way if He needed to. I wanted to listen to what God had to say to me and courageously share whatever He wanted me to share with others.

The only problem with listening to God was that if it was God's voice I was hearing, what He was saying didn't make sense. When I began to listen, I heard a clear voice in my spirit saying, "Trust Me." Now that seemed simple enough. But remember, I was out of a job, had a new baby (making a total of three children and a wife)—and the bills didn't just vanish! I knew that if I was hearing God correctly, He was saying, "Trust Me with your finances, future, bills, food, clothing, shelter, and family." He also said that I wasn't ready to minister. There was much more He wanted to teach me.

But wait a minute, Lord! Let me remind You, I have a Bible college degree, a master's of divinity, and 12 years of ministry experience. I preach, play guitar, sing, organize events, and so much more. And You're telling me I'm not ready to minister? But Lord, my résumé is awesome!

And God said, "Richard, you don't really even know Me." True, I didn't know His voice very well. But God was also telling me that my whole idea of ministry was wrong. He wanted me to trust Him and let Him retrain me.

What did I do? The same thing any rational, intelligent, hardworking American would do. Panic! I wrote up a résumé and hit every website looking for another ministry position. The voice I heard speaking to my spirit said, "Don't look for a job. I want to make you a disciple and teach you My ways."

But I replied, "That's not God! That's nuts! How can I pay my bills? How can I support my family? God, I've got talents and gifts that need to be used in a church somewhere. I've got bills to pay that won't just go away. How can I live on trust?"

For three months, God sustained us. I went on interviews and had churches offer me incredible salaries. They said I could write my own job description, they wanted me so much. But every time, I heard God saying, "If you want to follow Me, don't do it." During this time, people often came and brought us a check to cover the rent or our car payment. At the end of three months, our "income" equaled what I would have made working at a church.

I finally got up the courage to talk to Dawn about what was happening in my mind and spirit. I had wanted to hear God's voice, but the only thing I'd heard was "Trust Me and I'll supply all your needs. I, the Lord, want to teach you My ways." I was certain Dawn would be able to snap me out of this. After all, she was the sensible one. Wrong! Dawn said, "I know what you're saying is right. I've been hearing the same thing." Great! Now both of us were losing it.

By now I was in a very difficult position. I had no job, no title, and no money. I did have a great résumé, but the now-familiar voice was screaming in my ear: "Seek My face! Trust Me, and I will disciple you, lead you, and provide for you."

I began to wonder whether I was nuts. I knew the voice couldn't be God. All my life I'd been taught that I needed to work to earn a living. That was how God provided. It made no sense that God would want to waste all the training and gifts He had given me. But God said, "You don't even know Me. Some fishermen and tax collectors, a doctor, and some other guys knew more of Me than you do."

My pride was shattered. I wanted God to disciple me. I wanted Him to teach me ministry His way. But would God disciple me? For three years, Dawn and I had no salary at all. I was asked to preach many places, but we couldn't have lived on what was typically given. Some months we had $500 in regular support, and our monthly bills were several thousand dollars. After almost a year, we began to write a monthly letter to friends and family to tell them what God was teaching us. We made no appeals for money but simply let people know what God was doing.

People were often led to give us money. One businessman, an elder at his church, said that as he was flying home from a meeting, he was impressed by God to come straight to our house and deliver a check. As soon as he arrived home, he told his wife, got into his car, and drove over. He had heard God speak and wanted to obey. The gift he brought was exactly what we needed to pay our bills.

In three years, we were only late on our rent one time. All our bills were paid on time, except once when a check came two days late. That time the person told us that he couldn't sleep at night until he obeyed God. Not only was God speaking to me; He was speaking to many others about Dawn and me.

God also spoke to Dawn and me very specifically about giving to others. We were led to give away half our retirement and use the rest to pay off our van. Within days of obeying God, we received the same amount of money from some generous believers.

God also spoke to me on a regular basis through dreams and visions. I began to record the visions and dreams God was giving me.

God spoke very specific things to me when I was ministering to people. As I prayed for one friend, I actually saw him in an adulterous relationship.

Does God always speak to us? Many people who have been Christians for most of their lives say they've never heard God speak. They may have wrestled with the question of whether God really does speak today. That was true of me for most of my Christian life. Certainly there are many issues that prevent us from hearing God's voice. If we harbor sin, the Lord will not hear us (see Ps. 66:18). If we won't forgive others, it breaks our fellowship with God (see Mark 11:26). In First Samuel 8, we read the message of Samuel to the people of Israel when they begged for a king to rule them. God said that if He answered this request, they would face many hardships, and when they cried out to Him, He would not listen. How many times has God given us what we asked for, yet it brought leanness to our souls and damaged our fellowship with Him?

God longs for intimacy with us. He longs to be the center of our lives. He longs to speak with His people. Too often we're like the child who rushes into his father's room and demands something without taking the time to be with his dad. Have we ever fasted for any length of time so that we were dead to our own passions and emptied of self in order to truly listen? Fasting is not an exercise in self-torture. It's a blessing.

One issue is that fellowship has been broken between us and God. Another issue of equal importance is that we have not taken time to let God train us to discern His voice. There are many voices competing for our attention, and if we don't discipline ourselves to listen to Him, we may miss what He's telling us.

In Chapter 10, I will spend time laying a biblical foundation for hearing God's voice—a discipline very few Christians have developed. Many believers admit they hardly have time to listen to their spouses, who audibly and physically demand their attention! If we struggle to hear our spouses and children, we can expect to struggle with listening to God— that is, until it becomes a priority.

Study Questions

1. What are some of the ways God speaks today? Have you ever heard God speak to you apart from Scripture?

_____

_____

_____

_____

2. Have you had an experience, like Richard's, of hearing God speak to you but it didn't make sense to you, and in fact, it seemed like what you were hearing was totally crazy? What did you do?

_____

_____

_____

_____

3. What are some evidences that Richard really did hear God's voice and that God was intimately involved in the details of his life?

_____

_____

_____

4. What are some issues that could prevent us from hearing God's voice? (Read Psalm 66:18, Mark 11:26, and John 10:3-4.)

_____

_____

_____

5. How can we develop a greater intimacy with God and learn to hear His voice better?

_____

_____

_____

CHAPTER 4

Discipleship 101

O ne of the most familiar passages in the Bible—and one of my favorites—is Matthew 28:18-20, commonly known as the Great Commission:

> All authority in heaven and on earth has been given to Me. Therefore go and make disciples of all nations, baptizing them in the name of the Father and of the Son and of the Holy Spirit, and teaching them to obey everything I have commanded you. And surely I am with you always, to the very end of the age.

As I learned to listen to the Lord, I began to ask, "What is the *"everything I have commanded you"* that Jesus was referring to?" I had long been a student of discipleship and had seen hundreds of discipleship books that were filled with the "basics" believers should be grounded in—things like Scripture memorization, Bible reading, going to church, tithing, prayer, assurance of salvation, and more. I had often wondered who came up with what we consider the core essentials of discipleship—and how they came up with them. So I went to Scripture and asked God, "What's the *'everything I have commanded you'*?"

In the four Gospels, we find varying accounts of Jesus selecting 12 men He would train to be His disciples and eventually His apostles. The people He chose were average men with less-than-stellar credentials. These were the regular businesspeople of their day—men from all walks of life. Jesus didn't pick the Bible scholars, though some have suggested that Matthew was better trained than the rest. The fact is, these were ordinary men.

What did Jesus teach these disciples that they were supposed to teach to others? In three of the Gospels, we see the disciples watch Jesus heal the sick, cast out evil spirits, and preach the Kingdom of God. The next thing we see in each account is Jesus sending these same men out with an identical assignment. In Matthew 10, Mark 6, and Luke 9, Jesus sends out the original 12 disciples and gives them authority to do everything He had done. They were to heal the sick, cast out evil spirits, and preach the Kingdom of God. In Luke 10, Jesus sends out 72 disciples to cast out evil spirits, heal the sick, and preach about the Kingdom of God. In fact, this is the most clearly stated instruction Jesus gave His disciples. Could it be part of Jesus' method of making disciples? These three elements seem critical to what He wanted His followers to pass on to others.

Luke 10 raises another question about discipleship. Who were the 72 guys, and where did they come from? Had Jesus secretly set up a little school on the side? Were these the guys in whom the disciples were investing their lives to make disciples? This passage counters the teaching that this facet of ministry was reserved for the 12 apostles alone. Jesus was sending others to do the same things He'd taught the 12.

Then, in Acts, we see that even Stephen, a deacon, was doing miraculous signs and wonders. We see Paul picking up the same strategy used by Jesus and the apostles. In Acts 19, God used Paul to do extraordinary miracles. He healed the sick, cast out evil spirits, and even raised the dead (see Acts 20:7-12).

I had to be misinterpreting these passages since no one I knew had ever walked in or taught these things. In 34 years, I had never heard one sermon or lesson about healing. The same was true of casting out evil spirits. I had only heard of that happening in the deepest parts of Africa. With seven years of theological training, I couldn't have given you an intelligent answer about the Kingdom of God and what it entailed. I could give you the Four Spiritual Laws and several other presentations of the gospel, but were these the same as "the gospel of the Kingdom"—the message Jesus and the apostles preached? Was my understanding of the essentials of discipleship founded on God's model of discipleship—or on religious traditions passed down for generations?

If Jesus gave the model of discipleship, then I wasn't a disciple. The choice I faced was to redefine discipleship from what I could clearly see in Scripture or confess that I needed to start at the 101 level and let Jesus teach me. I began spending hours every day lying on my face with God's Word open. I fasted often and asked God Himself to disciple me. Not knowing anyone I could turn to about the things He was teaching me, I went straight to God.

Another disturbing truth God showed me during this time is that the word *Christian* is only found three times in the New Testament. Acts 11:26 (NASB) says, *"The disciples were first called Christians in Antioch."* In Acts 26:28, King Agrippa told Paul that Paul had almost persuaded him to become a Christian. And the third time the word *Christian* is used, Peter tells us, *"If you suffer as a Christian, do not be ashamed, but praise God that you bear that name"* (1 Pet. 4:16). The term *Christian* means "little Christ" or "follower of Christ." Because it comes from the Greek root word *Christ*, meaning "anointed," it could be translated "little anointed one."

I began to wonder how we came to have two different classifications of believers in the church. Today we seek to make Christians instead of disciples. But this is not what the Bible tells us to do. We've decided that for a radical few, we'll have discipleship—as if discipleship is an optional "second level" of spiritual life. Our practical theology (meaning what we do, not what we say) betrays the fact that we believe discipleship is optional. In fact, in most churches discipleship is not important enough that a coordinated program of discipleship is offered.

Of course, not even a program would suffice in making biblical disciples—yet programs are what we do in the church. Examining modern discipleship from the basis of Scripture, I saw that I could not defend any of the current discipleship models I knew of. If Jesus' methods provided the model for discipleship, then the key elements of the discipleship models I knew of were more basic and elementary than Jesus'—and the cost was not nearly what Jesus had laid out for His disciples.

I concluded that the church had lost the true biblical foundation for making disciples and had substituted a manmade approach. If this was the case, I wondered if it was even possible to experience "biblical discipleship." If what I was studying in God's Word was indeed what Jesus intended when He told us to teach "all" that He had taught, then I needed God to disciple me.

During this time, I received a call from my brother-in-law, asking me to speak at a college retreat. As I prepared for the retreat, I knew it was going to be special. I was beginning to trust that the voice I was hearing was God's, and that He was speaking to me. God told me I would see Him do things at the retreat I'd never seen before. That was exciting and filled me with anticipation. But the only thing I could imagine was more people raising their hands at the invitation!

In my first message, "Extreme Christianity," I challenged the students with the things God was teaching me. In Watchman Nee's book *The Normal Christian Life,* Nee explodes the myth of what "normal Christianity" is supposed to be. I had come to see that the "normal" faith we see in God's Word is extreme as compared with what is "normal" today. What the New Testament believers saw and did was extreme compared to what the church believes and experiences now. And what Jesus Himself expected from His disciples was extreme compared with what we expect today. Could it be that what we consider extreme is the normal expectation of God?

The students and I examined the New Testament and what God is calling and equipping His followers to do and be. Then, when I asked the students whether they wanted to sell out to the vision of extreme faith I had put before them, everyone in the group stood. They all wanted to be commissioned and prayed for as we began the retreat, so that God would help them sell out.

As I worked my way around the room, praying with individual students, an attractive young lady sat down and began to rock back and forth. She was breathing rapidly and loudly. As I got closer, she began to pull on her hair and shirt as if to rip it, and her rocking grew more violent. This had never happened when I spoke before, but I was certain this girl was manifesting demons. Some might have called it a seizure, but I didn't care what you called it. I wanted to know what to do!

Every eye in the room was glued to the scene as I silently prayed, "OK, God, I'm new at listening to You, but I need You to teach me really quickly what to do." Somehow I knew I should "plead the blood of Jesus," but I wasn't sure why that was important or what it was all about. I just did it. I also knew that there is power in Jesus' name, so I acted like I knew what I was doing and said something about the name of Jesus. Now what?

I sensed God leading me to do a few things I normally wouldn't think to do and then shout, "Freedom!" *But that's what TV evangelists do, isn't it, Lord?* There was no time to argue with God, so I shouted, "Freedom! In Jesus' name!" The girl went limp and looked around at all the faces staring at her. She was obviously embarrassed.

As I turned around and began to teach the group about what had just taken place, I hoped someone was taking good notes. The words I spoke were good, but they weren't from me. I didn't really know what had happened. No one had ever taught me about "setting captives free." Before that day, the blood of Jesus was just one of many theological components that had cognitive significance but no practical implication for ministry except for salvation. Now the name of Jesus was beginning to have a more powerful and practical application. Listening to God's Spirit was also growing in practical significance.

Later I sat with the girl while the others met in small groups. She told me she had chosen this church because "I knew the power of God wasn't here." She said that one other time she had gone to a church where something similar had happened. She knew that the power of God had caused the voices in her head to go crazy, and she had experienced a seizure at that church as well. Now she was going to psychotherapy and was on medication to silence the voices. She said that the peace she now felt was the first peace she could remember. The voices in her head were silent, and she felt God's presence and a joy and warmth she had never known before.

The girl said that when I'd begun to speak, she knew she was in trouble. She began to hear voices and had the urge to run out of the room. But the room was situated in such a way that from where she was seated, she couldn't have left without everyone noticing. She knew the power of God was present and that she wanted what I talked about, but she also wanted to run out screaming. Now she was free, at peace, and excited about what lay ahead.

Talk about a powerful way to start a retreat! The students were on fire. Only 35 students came to that retreat, but several of them still point to it and a subsequent mission trip I led in Tampa, Florida, as the time when God called them into full-time Christian ministry. They wanted New Testament Christianity, and this was the closest they had ever come. Ironically, it was also the closest I had come!

This was my first encounter with the demonic, but it wasn't my last. What followed was a six-month period in which every time I spoke at a retreat or led worship, someone would begin manifesting demons. All of these encounters happened in Baptist churches among people who had been in church for years. I began to ask God to teach me more so I could really help these people. With each encounter, I was learning new things.

One book that ministered to me during this time was *Healing Through Deliverance* by Peter Horrobin. The author was from England, and he had also seen in the Gospels Jesus' pattern of discipleship and become a lifelong student and teacher of the ministry of healing, deliverance, and the Kingdom of God. Horrobin's organization, Ellel Ministries, has trained tens of thousands from all over the world in this vital ministry. His book examines thoroughly every biblical reference to the ministry of setting captives free.

It was critical for me to have this type of biblical foundation since I had been trained to develop a biblical theology. What disturbed me was the fact that I'd been in church every time the doors were open for over 30 years. I had studied at some of the best schools for seven years to get degrees that would make me an expert. But in all my life, I had never heard a single sermon or Bible study on healing, casting out evil spirits, or the Kingdom of God. The only book I was required to read on this matter came during my final year of seminary. It was Neil Anderson's *The Bondage Breaker*. I had also read *The Adversary* by Mark I. Bubeck. Apart from these two books, I had no knowledge of these activities—foundational elements of Jesus' ministry, as well as of the ongoing ministry of the disciples.

If this was Jesus' pattern of discipleship, then the Church desperately needed to regain the truths that had been robbed from her. Not only did I want to be discipled; I wanted to make as many disciples as I could and teach them to disciple others! Already I was sharing everything God was teaching me with anyone who would listen. I shared the truths I was learning with several pastor friends and asked them to show me if I was wrong. The interaction with them was helpful, and their questions and challenges sharpened my thinking and caused me to dig deeper. Yet I had no idea how much impact these interactions were having on them and their ministries. Though many friends in ministry rejected what I was saying, some joined me in my quest for biblical discipleship. And as you'll soon see, the impact of our regaining these truths became enormous in our city.

My earnest prayer is that the Church throughout the world will regain a biblical foundation for discipleship. If we get back to Jesus' strategy, millions will find freedom.

Study Questions

1. Read Matthew 28:18-20. Jesus says, *"... Teaching them to obey everything I have commanded you...."* What did Jesus teach His disciples?

_____

_____

_____

2. Read Matthew 10:1, 5-8; Mark 6:6-7, 12-13; and Luke 9:1-2. What were the main things Jesus was teaching His disciples to do?

_____

_____

_____

3. Are there two different classifications of believers: first-level Christians and second-level disciples? Why or why not?

_____

_____

_____

4. If the things that are discussed in this chapter are indeed foundations of discipleship, have you been discipled? Is your church making biblical disciples?

_____

_____

_____

5. Do you want to become a biblical disciple and learn to do the things that Jesus taught His disciples to do?

_____

_____

_____

CHAPTER 5

Class 201—The Pursuit of Discipleship

For the next year, I spent hours each day on my face in prayer, diligently studying God's Word. These were the best of days and the worst of days. Often I wrestled with the nagging question of whether I'd gone crazy. Everything I was learning seemed so clear in Scripture, but I had heard none of it in church or seminary. Why not? Also, I had no job, position, or title—things that typically define a man's identity—yet somehow God was supplying what my family needed. How long would God continue to supply our needs? Every month I would struggle between doubt and faith in God's provision for the month ahead.

Several groups asked me to preach at revival meetings or lead worship on retreats. For the first time in my life, God's power was becoming real to me. There was a new fire in my heart, and God's Word was coming to life as never before. I saw more fruit when I spoke than in all my previous years of ministry. Pastors and leaders where I ministered acknowledged that God was doing something powerful; they too saw the fruit of God in the lives of people when I ministered. But often what happened deviated enough from their sense of the norm that some wouldn't ask me back. It's not that what happened was weird, freaky, or bad; in each case, someone was set free or healed. Yet when unfamiliar things begin to happen—things outside their frame of reference—it was disturbing. I was amazed at how much opposition can arise when God begins to work in power in our lives.

If you pursue biblical discipleship, you too will likely experience persecution and rejection. People may falsely speak evil of you. But many more will tell you that their lives have been radically and eternally changed through your ministry. When God uses you to set a captive free or heals someone as you pray, you'll experience incredible satisfaction and often deep gratitude from those touched by your prayer—and this will more than make up for those who've rejected you.

In Matthew 5, Jesus told us to expect persecution and view it as an honor. I always expected this kind of persecution to come from nonbelievers. But in Jesus' own ministry, He was usually rejected by the members of the religious community who did not believe what He taught or experience what He lived.

Powerful Encounters

At one retreat, I was asked to chaperone and lead worship for a Baptist youth group. Two amazing things happened that week. First, I didn't expect to be paid anything, and on Friday as we were getting ready to leave, Dawn and I had prayed for a supernatural provision of a thousand dollars—exactly the amount needed to pay our bills on Monday.

As I boarded the bus, someone told me there was a person outside who wanted to see me. I got off the bus, and there stood the mother of one of the students. She told me that for over a week, God had told her and her husband to give something to our ministry, and that they had been putting it off. She handed me an envelope, we hugged, and I climbed back on the bus. When I opened the envelope, there was a check for $1,000! I climbed off the bus and made a beeline for the phone inside the church to let Dawn know God had answered our prayers again.

Another powerful encounter with God occurred one evening during worship. God's presence was particularly palpable that evening, and in the middle of worship, two girls ran out of the room. Several students and a few staff followed them out, and within a matter of minutes, one of the college-age staff came back in—his eyes wide—and asked me to come immediately.

Turning the worship over to another leader, I followed him to a room where it sounded like a girl was giving birth to a baby. The leaders informed me that the girl had lost feeling in half of her body. As I entered the room, she lay there in the fetal position, holding her stomach and screaming in pain. The leaders had discerned that this girl's issues were spiritual more than physical, which in itself is amazing, since none of them had witnessed anything like this before, and most people would have called for an ambulance.

We began to pray for and minister to this girl and sought to discern the strongholds in her life. This was only the third time I had encountered something like this; I was only several months into this new discipleship process and desperately wished for someone else to deal with the situation so that I could watch and learn from him or her. But God gave me wisdom and direction, and in a matter of minutes, the young lady was free. I began to wonder if this was going to begin happening every time I spoke or led worship. It was very unsettling, and it sometimes made pastors uncomfortable! Some expressed concerns that I was becoming too "charismatic."

It's amazing how often believers label and categorize what they don't understand. I believe that to write off something simply because it's outside our realm of experience is to limit God—and ultimately, to keep the Church from experiencing God. The typical argument of the so-called "experts" is that people who begin to experience the supernatural are in danger of basing their theology on experience. I have come to see that the "experts" I used to read and believe are basing their theology on what they haven't experienced. If Jesus did it and taught His disciples to do it, then it was good enough for me.

I would challenge you to examine the label "charismatic," which comes from the Greek word *charisma,* which means "gift of grace." Our salvation is a gift of grace. Spiritual gifts are gifts of grace. We don't earn them or deserve them, but God gives them anyway. All believers accept God's gift of salvation, and most believe that God gives spiritual gifts. So how could something so beautiful come to be a derogatory label?

When we think of the word *charismatic,* various images often come to mind. One might think of lively music, hands raised, joy, and vibrancy in worship. Another thinks of the TV evangelist who seems to be a charlatan and is out to take people's money, or people shaking and acting like God is all over them but going out and living like the devil. Some envision people pressuring them to pray in tongues and telling them they're not saved if they don't.

Labels carry a variety of connotations for each of us. We seek to put people into categories that make sense to us. Then we judge them according to those categories.

All black people are…

All white people are…

All fat people are…

All short people are…

All skinny people are…

Perhaps you have a natural tendency to finish one of these sentences a certain way. That tendency is dangerous, and it keeps the Body of Christ divided.

Some of you may have labeled this book while reading the first chapter. I would caution against that. All I have described has come from repeated encounters with the living God. Nothing happened because I went to a new church, seminar, or training course. This fresh encounter with God was born of much prayer, fasting, and study of Scripture. God began to remove the labels I held in my heart, and I looked at the Word of God without the lenses that used to shade its meaning to suit my denomination and personal bias.

Have you embraced the labels Christians tend to put on believers of a different stripe? Do you write people off when what they say doesn't fit what you've been told all your life? Can you accept the fact that your experience or lack thereof should not be the basis of what you believe and accept? It's critical that you not even accept what I say based upon my experience. Compare what you read with the Word of God. It has to line up. Truth, however, does not have to line up with what we've been taught or with our traditions—unless, of course, those foundations are truly biblical.

I didn't know what to call it when God began to work in power in my life and ministry, but I did know that I liked it. You could call me anything you wanted—charismatic, crazy, or fanatical. I liked knowing that my ministry was now more in line with New Testament ministry, like what the apostles did in Acts. I liked seeing people receive freedom through God's power, rather than becoming dependent on me for long-term counseling. Even the persecution was acceptable when I realized that persecution was normal for a disciple.

People began to hear stories about what was happening, and phone calls started to come my way. A deacon from a Baptist church wanted me to meet with and pray for his daughter, who was getting out of the hospital where she'd been treated for mental problems. The man and his wife were literally afraid for their lives as they brought her back into their home. They had installed deadbolts on all of their bedroom doors to keep their own daughter out of their rooms. The girl had been hearing voices,

clawing herself, and seeing two spirits who often talked to her. The man
had heard me praying a short prayer at his church one Sunday morning
and thought perhaps I'd be able to help her.

For two hours one night we ministered to the girl and saw God mi-
raculously heal and set her free. The fears she had lived with for most of
her life were gone. The girl had been a victim of sexual abuse for years
at the hands of her own brother and his friends. Her mother had died
when she was only seven, and since that time, she had seen spirits that
tormented her.

As I share testimonies like this when I speak, I'm amazed at how many
people come up and tell me about their own inner torment. Men and
women regularly approach me and tell of the voices they hear and the
things they see. Perhaps as you're reading this book, you've begun to feel
a sense of hope. You've shared your experiences with others, and they've
looked at you like you were crazy. Perhaps you told a counselor and were
sent to someone who could prescribe medication. You hate the fears and
the torment, but you've learned to cope. Many of you are church leaders,
ministers, and pastors' wives. Some of you gave up hope of ever finding
relief from the inner torment. Let me assure you: You can be free! We at
Operation Light Force minister to hundreds and hundreds of people a
year and see them healed and set free. We are constantly training people
to minister in the power of God and set others free.

One family called to say that they were experiencing many strange
things in their house. They were involved in leadership at a church but
had told no one about the things they were experiencing. They thought
people would think they were crazy. I became used to conversations that
began, "I've never told anyone about this before, but—" or "You're probably going to think I'm crazy, but—." For some it was nightmares, hearing voices, or seeing things, while for others it was suicidal thoughts,
overwhelming depression, rage, or fear. People began to contact us with
their need for physical healing. They had tried medicine and were given
no hope of healing. I was and am still amazed at the amount of torment

people lived with. Many thought it normal to face the things they were facing. Parents whose children had nightmares every night figured it was normal. They had no idea that what their children experienced night after night could be stopped by the power of God. No one had ever told them that there's hope of freedom from whatever the torment.

In one year, I saw and heard more demonic activity than in my entire life, and I began to realize that this was an untouched facet of ministry in the church. We didn't look for it, but in church after church, whenever the subject presented itself, people came forward, practically begging for ministry. These were not natives from the dark recesses of Africa. They were pastors, youth pastors, deacons, elders, and lay leaders in solid churches across America.

I began to wonder how much demonic activity was present in our churches on a weekly basis, while the Church sat back powerless, with a theology that gave more credence to modern counseling and drugs than to the power of God. In the places where I was ministering, individuals and families were finding freedom. I knew so little, but God was gracious to lead me by the hand. It would be several years before a real breakthrough would come and this discipleship model would expand to the next level of equipping others. Eventually we would make this training available for the world through our website, www.operationlightforce.com. For now, I was simply learning from Jesus what it meant to be a disciple.

Christians and Counseling

Perhaps you've wondered as you've read this chapter whether there is any benefit in believers going to professional counselors when they are tormented by fear, anxiety, depression, and other negative thoughts. Let me be clear that God uses counselors in the lives of many people and that counseling indeed has a place in the Body of Christ. I do believe that there are certain strongholds from which you cannot counsel a person free. I've seen people who have been going to counselors for years, who are stuck in the same place where they began. When they have received ministry for freedom from demonic strongholds and oppression, they've been radically transformed and set free from things that the best counselors could not help them escape.

What I have found in these instances is that the individual being counseled found it impossible to apply good counsel because there was a spiritual force holding him or her captive. Once the spiritual bondage was dealt with, the person was enabled to apply the great counsel given. You cannot counsel a demon out of a person's life. Many people don't consider the possibility of the demonic because they don't believe that a Christian can be in bondage to demons. Later in this book, I will address the question of whether Christians can be oppressed by demons.

Great Commission Ministry

Jesus made disciples by equipping them to set free those in bondage to sin and the demonic and to break free of these strongholds. He equipped them to heal the sick. And He taught His disciples about the Kingdom of God. The Great Commission commands us to teach those we disciple everything Jesus taught His disciples. Therefore, two of the key objectives in fulfilling the Great Commission are to set captives free and to teach other disciples how to do this. Another aspect of Jesus' discipleship program that is lacking today is healing the sick. Jesus sent out the 12 and the 72, telling them to heal the sick. There is much to learn from Scripture that can help us pray more effectively for healing. But we won't learn about this important subject if we fail to study it because of a denominational bias against healing or a tendency to stereotype those who engage in this aspect of ministry. If we are neglecting to teach disciples any part of the "everything" Jesus taught, then our discipleship today will be lacking.

I strongly urge you to check out our website, www.operationlight-force.com, for more discipleship training in the things that Jesus dealt with in regard to healing, setting captives free, and preaching the Kingdom of God.

Study Questions

1. Why is it possible to go to church all your life and never hear a sermon about healing, casting out evil spirits, or any of a number of subjects that are found throughout God's Word?

   _____

   _____

   _____

2. Why would people who profess to be believers persecute others who are diligently pursuing to know what God's Word teaches about these subjects?

   _____

   _____

   _____

3. How many people do you know in churches today who are in serious bondage to all types of problems? Is God not able to set people free, or have we failed to know God's power and be able to minister in His power?

   _____

   _____

   _____

4. Have you ever seen someone you believe was being tormented by evil spirits? Have you ever been tormented? What was that like?

_____

_____

_____

5. Do you believe that the Church today needs to recapture this facet of ministry? If you do, what will you do?

_____

_____

_____

CHAPTER 6

Unsung Heroes and Kingdom Lessons

As I was learning to hear God's voice and asking Jesus to disciple me, the Lord led me to continue ministering in the inner city. Dawn and I attended various churches, and though both of us had been to church every week since childhood, we felt strongly led that our home group, which met on Sunday nights, was to become our primary place of fellowship for the next year or two. Many close friends in ministry gave no encouragement regarding the things God was teaching me. These men and their opinions had mattered a lot to me, and it was with deep pain that I was led by God to back away. God was telling me that, for me, if I was going to be discipled I had, for a while, to leave behind all I had come to know, love, and find my identity in.

Dawn and I felt as if we were in a spiritual no man's land. Most of our former friends in ministry still loved us but could not accept what God was doing in our lives. Some were fairly harsh in their assessment and advice. Some mocked the walk of faith and the fasting. Others couldn't believe any of the miracles that were happening came from God or believe the stories because they didn't fit their belief system. Though I loved and respected them, I knew God was leading me and working in our lives.

One friend illustrated what was happening like this: When a child begins to draw with crayons, he colors all over the page. His color choices are less than perfect, and he doesn't stay inside the lines. But when he brings you the picture, you say, "That's beautiful!" You know that he won't always color such messes, and you speak encouragement so that he'll want to color more. You may point out the lines and suggest the right colors, but for the most part, you realize that he'll improve over time and eventually color well—inside the lines and with the right colors.

In the early days, I had no one to teach me how to color inside the lines. Sometimes it was messy, but I was a baby disciple with much to learn. I could put up with some criticism, and I let that criticism shape me and challenge me to be sure everything I was learning lined up with God's Word.

Inner-City Ministry

On Saturday mornings, our family would go down to an inner-city ministry that fed as many as 200 homeless people. They began with a time of worship and a message from God's Word and then opened up the food lines. God told me clearly to not tell them I could preach or sing. He said, *"Just put food on the plates and look into the eyes of those you're serving."* He said I would see Jesus in their eyes. I began to talk with the men and hear their stories. I saw the hurt, pain, and rejection that consumed these people.

Every other week I saw someone who didn't fit the crowd. One week it was a teenager with clean, white Nikes. Another week it was a sharply dressed young lady or someone who looked better suited for a downtown office. All these people were running from something or controlled by some addiction.

One morning a man showed up looking lost. I came to find out, John had just been released from the United States Penitentiary in Leavenworth, Kansas. For 30 years, he'd been locked away for a crime he'd committed at age 17. While in prison John had become a Christian, earned a bachelor's degree, become certified as an electrician as well as in heating and air conditioning, and had become the lead maintenance man at the prison.

John's family had rejected him years ago, and he didn't even know where they lived. All he knew was that he used to live in Tampa, so that's where he headed. He had been in Tampa for three days and was looking for work and a place to live. Several of us reached out to John and helped him find a job, an apartment, and a church. The stories John told us would break your heart. Here he was at age 47, and nearly two-thirds of his life had been spent in a penitentiary. That was the only life he knew. John was scared, but God reached out to him. This kind of story was repeated many times by the "unsung heroes" of our city—the people who served week after week in this ministry.

On Wednesday nights I was led to go to a small church in the inner city. Again God told me to sit in the back, keep my mouth shut, and learn. I watched a group of 50 to 60 believers ministering in this crack-infested neighborhood, serving with uncharacteristic love and abandon.

Ed Bunting had integrated the neighborhood when he moved in. Four years before I met him, Ed had been the manager of the largest nightclub in Tampa. He had hired the strippers and musicians, overseen the finances, and managed every other facet of the business—that is, until he went to Promise Keepers and gave his life to Christ. Ed immediately saw the conflict between his occupation and his newfound faith. So he decided to turn his nightclub into a Christian nightclub. He proceeded to fire all the dancers, get rid of the alcohol, and play Christian music. Many people didn't like the changes, including the owner. Needless to say, Ed soon found himself unemployed.

Ed began to wonder what God's will was for his life. He focused his energy on starting another Christian nightclub, and with his connections and background, the club was an instant success. It didn't take long for Ed to question this approach when he saw Christians cheat on their wives and believers dancing just like those at the previous clubs he had managed and acting very much like unbelievers.

Again Ed found himself unemployed. Seeing in Scripture that God cared about the hungry, the naked, and the lonely, Ed figured God wanted him to minister to the homeless. Ed didn't know anyone who paid people to do this, but he poured everything he had into reaching out and helping guys get their lives together. When the pastor of a small, inner-city church offered him a trailer next to the church, Ed moved in and began to serve the church and reach out to the homeless. He took guys in to live in the trailer and helped them get jobs, get right with God, and deal with the many problems they faced.

Scripture is clear that God's people are to care for the fatherless, feed the hungry, clothe the naked, bind up the brokenhearted, and bring liberty to those who are captive. Yet the majority of those who claim the name of Christ never do a single thing. Paul told the Philippians that the money they supplied to him caused them to become partakers in the same spiritual blessing he had received. The most powerful way you can fulfill God's Word in this manner is to go on a regular basis and volunteer. It will change your life. You can also support these ministries financially. These people spend so much time serving that they seldom ask for support. Thus nearly every inner-city ministry that is making a significant impact has very little money. I challenge you to find an inner-city ministry to support with both your time and your finances. You will fulfill God's Word, but more than that, you'll be transformed and used of God to minister to others.

Another unsung hero was a woman named Nelia. We nicknamed Nelia "the Debutante." She had obviously come from money and had a thick Tennessee accent. Nelia was from Memphis and had both come from wealth and been the wife of a wealthy lawyer. Her husband forced her to choose between Christ and him, and though Nelia tried to hold her marriage together, she would not leave Christ. Finding herself divorced, Nelia was led by God to Tampa. She knew only one person in Tampa but came in obedience to God. God had told her she would have a ministry in Tampa.

When Nelia and David Jones, pastor of the little inner-city church, met for the first time, David offered Nelia a place to live next to the church—on the other side from Ed, in a house we affectionately called "the roach motel." Nelia soon began to serve the little church, as well as the crack-infested neighborhood that surrounded it. She began to take in girls who had once been strippers or drug addicts or were running away. She spent whole nights with them—praying over them, ministering deliverance to them, serving and teaching them.

As I sat in the back of this little church, I began to get to know its members—and the Lord would ask me questions. He'd say, *Are the pastors of the big church you served in, whose names are written in books, more important than these? Does their faith or yours compare to the faith of the believers in this little church?* The Christians in this church would gather five days a week at 6:00 A.M., praying for revival in the city. They prayed until noon every day. There might be 8 to 20 people there, depending on what time it was. People came for two hours before the workday began— or on their day off from work. God was humbling me greatly. I had been so arrogant. I thought I had so much to offer, and God was showing me how many limitations there were in my faith, love, and devotion to Him. He was also showing me that, as Paul described in Second Timothy 3:5, I had a form of godliness that denied the power. In fact, I had redefined what power was so that verses like that would not convict me.

I had come to define success in ministry as large numbers, big budgets, tons of programs, grandiose facilities, and a big salary. The church I had come from had all that. I had been living "the American Church Dream"! We had copied all the formulas of the mega churches and even improved on many of them. People flocked to hear the professional-sounding band, watch the light show and drama, and get a message that would help them with their marriages, finances, raising children, or any of the other issues they faced in life. With so much activity, it was hard to stop and face the facts. Many of those who had been through all the seminars, small groups, and support groups and heard all the sermons were still getting divorced, still overmedicated, still not feeding the hungry, caring for orphans, or defending the fatherless. There was no power of God operating and little or no freedom.

The churches I had been involved with were revolving doors. People went out as fast as they came in. Sure, at peak times of the year there were 2,000 attending, but people flowed in and out like water through a sieve. Why? What were they looking for that they didn't find? Could there be more? We were often too overtaxed to take time to ask those questions. When we did, they overwhelmed us—because who had time to add another program to the schedule? A new program was always the answer. There had to be a program to fix the problem we faced.

We had a huge counseling center, 10 full-time pastors, 15 office personnel, and more. My youth budget alone had been close to $40,000, including the $10,000 we raised each year at our auction. We got to the place where we didn't need prayer. When you get enough clever programs and a big enough budget, when you get good at marketing and packaging the product, you can leave God out of the equation. You may think I'm overstating my case, but it's nearly impossible when you're in that programmatic track to stop and take an honest look at where you're headed.

When Jesus wrote to the churches in Revelation, it was a letter from the greatest lover of all time. Jesus had just laid down His life for this Bride of His. He was in Heaven, preparing a place for her. In that context, read Revelation 3:15-17:

> *I know your deeds, that you are neither cold nor hot. I wish you were either one or the other! So, because you are lukewarm—neither hot nor cold—I am about to spit you out of My mouth. You say, "I am*

rich; I have acquired wealth and do not need a thing." But you do not realize that you are wretched, pitiful, poor, blind and naked.

Jesus doesn't mince words here. In verse 19, He says, *"Those whom I love I rebuke and discipline."* Well, it sure is good to be loved, but does the spanking have to hurt so much? God had convicted me that my whole measuring stick of success was nothing like His. My ministry had been devoid of His power. I had prayed more than many of my peers, but I didn't pray with great effect. I had actually been blind to much of what God wanted from me and from His Church. God was not nearly as impressed with our church growth as we were. Size and activities didn't score as many points with Him as it did in the eyes of man. Who had we been trying to please anyway?

Have you come to the place in your life and ministry where you know there must be more? Do the words I'm sharing make you angry? Are you feeling threatened because what you've done and believed as a Christian is being questioned? Rather than taking my words personally, take them as a challenge. What will it hurt if you take some time to stop, get really quiet, and listen? Can you hear the still, small voice of the Master? He longs to be intimate with you. He longs to disciple you because He loves you.

Jesus was giving me a new way of measuring success in ministry. He was showing me people who had found real riches and true joy in serving the King. I had watched so many church leaders who were miserable—controlled by greed and a love for power. I had seen the emptiness that comes from ministry driven by pride and the desire to be biggest and best. I had repeatedly seen spiritual leaders devour one another and destroy the lives of those who would question their method or challenge them.

As God showed me simple people who ministered out of a pure heart, gave everything for the sake of the Kingdom, and cared nothing about the size of their paycheck as long as Jesus was pleased, I knew I had tasted the Kingdom of God. I was among those who are poor in spirit, to whom the Kingdom of Heaven belongs (see Matt. 5:3).

As I listened to the Lord and saw things with eyes that had been opened, I realized that these "unsung heroes" were the freest people I had ever met. They had joy, peace, and love. None of them were medicated due to the stress of their ministry. They didn't have big buildings or big budgets, but they had the deeper things that many believers seek, long for, strive for, and find so elusive. They had found the pearl of great price. Jesus said:

> The kingdom of heaven is like a treasure hidden in a field. When a man found it, he hid it again, and then in his joy went and sold all he had and bought that field. Again, the kingdom of heaven is like a merchant looking for fine pearls. When he found one of great value, he went away and sold everything he had and bought it (Matthew 13:44-46).

I too had found the Kingdom of God and had come to realize that it was worth everything I owned. It was worth everything I had given up and more. If someone had offered me a million dollars, it would not have kept me from pursuing the Kingdom of God.

Have you found the Kingdom of God, or are you chasing a substitute? Can you say with all sincerity that you have the joy of the Lord? Are you experiencing the *"peace of God, which surpasses all understanding"* (Phil. 4:7 NKJV)? When you encounter a person who is in bondage to addiction, fear, or depression, do you have confidence that you can set him free? When you pray for the sick, are they normally healed, or is that a rare-to-never occurrence?

Don't let the answers to these questions discourage you. Let them invigorate you with a fresh desire to be discipled by Jesus. You may have to resign your frantic pace in order to enter Jesus' school of discipleship. You may need to get a new idea of what success is. Some of your present heroes may reject you, but you'll meet new "unsung heroes." You'll discover that these people may not have the worldly trappings of success, but they've experienced the deeper things of God—His joy, His peace, His power, and victory. You cannot put a price on these.

Study Questions

1. Who are some unsung heroes you know about? What makes them heroes?

_____

_____

_____

2. Read Second Timothy 3:1-5. How indicative is that passage of many Christians today? Do we have a form of godliness that denies the power?

_____

_____

_____

3. Read Revelation 3:15-17. How did Laodicean Christians view themselves? How did Jesus view them? Why were their perspectives so different?

_____

_____

_____

4. Have you come to the place in your life and ministry where you know there must be more?

_____

_____

_____

5. Have you found the Kingdom of God, or are you chasing a substitute? Are you living in peace and the joy of the Lord? Do you have the confidence to set captives free? Are the sick healed when you pray? How do these questions make you feel? Why?

_____

_____

_____

CHAPTER 7

Into the Desert—Knocked Off My Horse

P raise God that He was gracious enough to begin transforming this well-educated, self-righteous Pharisee. I could now understand what Paul must have felt when he was knocked off his horse, blinded by the light, and actually heard God speak to him. What I had believed was the path to successful ministry was, in reality, a road that led away from God. The very things I had opposed because of my theological training and my quickly crumbling God box were some of the most essential elements of a biblical ministry.

I remembered praying a prayer while I was at Calvary Church during a study of *The Making of a Leader* by Bobby Clinton and *Experiencing God* by Henry Blackaby. I had prayed that God would allow me to experience the desert type of teaching experience that God had given the apostle Paul. After Paul was thrown from his horse, he heard the voice of God while his companions did not. Just hearing God speak no doubt rattled his theological cage! Blindness covered his eyes until he met a follower of "the Way," as believers were called at that time. The man, whom Paul would have been out to kill, was named Ananias. Ananias healed Paul's blindness, just as the voice that claimed to be God had said he would.

After this encounter, Paul spent several years in the desert, being taught by the Holy Spirit. When Paul left the desert, he ministered in the power of God, wrote much of the New Testament, and transformed cities and nations. To fully comprehend Paul's teaching in the Epistles, you must keep this background in mind. Paul's teaching cannot be understood apart from remembering what was going on in his life. It wasn't just prison, shipwrecks, and speaking. When Paul ministered, God showed up and demonstrated His power through Paul—even to the point that *"...handkerchiefs and aprons that had touched him were taken to the sick, and their illnesses were cured and the evil spirits left them"* (Acts 19:12). It says in Acts 19 that Paul did extraordinary miracles. Until this new season of my life, I hadn't even seen ordinary miracles, much less the extraordinary variety.

There were many instances in which Paul healed the sick and cast out evil spirits. Paul was also used by God to raise the dead:

> *Seated in a window was a young man named Eutychus, who was sinking into a deep sleep as Paul talked on and on. When he was sound asleep, he fell to the ground from the third story and was picked up dead. Paul went down, threw himself on the young man and put his arms around him. "Don't be alarmed," he said. "He's alive!"* (Acts 20:9-10).

God worked mightily in the lives of the apostles throughout the written history of the Church. Why did this stop? I had been taught that God limited Himself to working in this way through the apostles. Many have tried to build a scriptural foundation for this belief, but there is no biblical basis for the notion that God ever ceased this type of ministry. What we have done is develop a theology to support our experiences or lack of experiences. We do this so we can feel good about our faith even though it falls far short of what we see in the Word of God. Since beginning this journey with the Lord, I have been privileged to see most of the miracles in the Bible, but it is funny how many from my old school of theology would say that my belief system was based on my experience.

The opposite is true. My experience has been radically transformed by my belief system. My belief system changed to a more biblical belief system before I experienced anything.

I had wanted to become a transformer, but I didn't know how to get there. Recalling my prayer asking God to teach me in a "desert" experience, I asked God if what I was going through was perhaps the answer to that prayer. Somehow I knew it was! Then, half seriously, I asked Him if I could retract that prayer. After all, it wasn't until later in Paul's life that he counted everything he had lost as rubbish. I still missed having a nice salary, the respect of my peers, and a position in a prestigious church. The trappings around me were less than glamorous. People who used to love me no longer returned my calls and said hurtful things about me to others that found their way back to me. I was in a desert, but I was learning— not just filling my head. I was experiencing God's Word as it is for today. I was having my character shaped and reshaped.

Paul was fairly young when God knocked him from his horse and started him on a new course. He was the rising star among the Pharisees. The best scholars had trained him, he had the perfect pedigree, and he had an uncommon zeal that had been noticed by no less than the high priest himself. If he wasn't already receiving a substantial wage for his service, he surely would have once he finished his deadly task of eliminating "the Way." Paul had an official title given to him. He had a job that was created just for him by the top religious leader of the day. He was headed straight for the top and going there fast. Paul may likely have become the next candidate for the high priest's office. Can you imagine what his zeal would have produced for evil?

At that time in my life, Paul was the character I identified with most. I had no salary. I realized that despite seven years of rigorous theological training, I didn't know the 101-level material Jesus had taught His freshmen class. I had once been "Director of Student Ministries" at one of the fastest-growing churches in America. A national church consultant had told our pastor that I was the "dark horse" on his staff of ten pastors. I was the lowest man; one day I would be "the star." Some kind of star I was now, putting food on the plates of homeless people and sitting on the back row of an inner-city Tampa church, being humbled by the lives and ministry of some people nobody knew existed—making no money, having no job, no title, and very little direction.

There were still many days when I asked myself, *How could this be God?* I figured Moses must have asked the same question many times as he journeyed in the desert. Churches continued to offer me jobs and practically begged me to come and work with their youth. One pastor called several times a week and took me out to dinner with the wealthiest man I had ever met. Though I tried to scare him off with stories of what God was doing in my life, he was fine with it and still wanted me to come to his church. Inside, I wanted to accept the position and the money and go back to what I knew. But I couldn't go back. I had heard God and been thrown from my horse. I had seen Jesus, and now I was walking a new path.

It was hard to explain to anyone. Like Abraham, I knew God had called me to go. I knew He was leading me. I couldn't tell you where I was going because I didn't know myself. I couldn't say how to get there, but I knew God was leading. Deep inside, I knew that I was saner than I had ever been, even though most of my friends and former colleagues in ministry may have debated this.

It's actually the grace of God that would knock someone off his course in life and offer him His course and His mission. God is the God of second chances, and He seeks to call us to join His vision. Often when we're praying for God to bless our vision or mission, God is trying to get our attention and call us back to His. We tend to think our mission is His Mission and our vision is His Vision, but too often we aren't listening. We do all the talking.

God is calling the Church in America back to His Vision and His Mission. He is calling the Church back to biblical discipleship—to preaching the Kingdom, the power of God for healing, and the ministry of casting out evil spirits.

Has God ever taken you through a desert experience, where you came to question everything you once held to be true? Have you ever been confronted by the reality that you taught things you believed to be true but then discovered that they were not only untrue but detrimental to others? It's almost as profound an experience as conversion. In fact, it is a type of conversion. When we are converted, we repent from turning away from God with our life to running after God. In my case, like Paul, I had thought I was serving God, when in actuality I had been working against God many times. Now I was in His school, following His instructions. It was like starting over, but it was awesome.

The Dream and the Woman

Before I share the following dream, it's important that you realize what God's Word says about dreams. God spoke to many people throughout Scripture in dreams: Abimelech in Genesis 20, Jacob in Genesis 28 and 31, Laban in Genesis 31, Joseph in Genesis 37, a pagan cupbearer and a baker in Genesis 40, Pharaoh in Genesis 41, Gideon overhears the dreams of his enemy in Judges 7, Solomon in First Kings 3, Nebuchadnezzar in Daniel 2, Joseph in Matthew 1 and 2, and Pilate's wife in Matthew 27. This is not a complete list but represents the breadth and variety of God given dreams that run throughout Scriptures.

Many times the Word of God says that God came to a certain person in a dream. There are no instances of dreams in Scripture not coming from God, but Jeremiah warns against prophets who prophesy lies in telling of their dreams (see Jer. 23:25-28). A dream does not have the veracity of Scripture. The prophet makes that inference in Jeremiah 23:28 when he likens the Word of God to wheat and dreams to straw. Yet compared with the number of times God spoke very specific things to His people in dreams, there are very few warnings about them in Scripture.

God has also spoken to His people throughout history in visions. Scripture actually provides more instances of God speaking in visions than in dreams. When God gives a vision, it's unmistakable. Visions can be as vivid as dreams. The only difference is that you're fully awake. Some have visions when their eyes are closed and they are praying, while some see visions with their eyes open. God's Word promised that in the last days God would pour out His Spirit and His people would see visions and dreams (see Joel 2 and Acts 2). The majority of Scripture passages about visions are clearly in favor of God speaking to His people, especially His prophets, through visions. There are also warnings in both Jeremiah and Ezekiel about those who would prophesy lies, telling of visions from their own minds.

It is important to avoid both errors. On the one hand, it's wrong to dismiss dreams and visions and not allow them to be shared. But on the other hand, it is always critical to weigh them against Scripture. Even Scripture must be weighed. People use God's Word for their own means and take it out of context. Just because someone uses the Bible incorrectly doesn't mean we throw out the Bible. In the same way, don't despise dreams or visions.

One night God spoke to me in a dream. I was headed for Argentina to spend 19 days working with Ed Silvoso and Harvest Evangelism in a massive outreach to that nation. A team of about eight from Tampa was spending the night in a Miami hotel.

In my dream, I was traveling across America when we stopped for gas. I needed to wash my hands and asked the attendant where the restroom was. The man told me to go out the backdoor into the next building, head to the left, and go to another door at the rear. The man then told me to ignore the woman I would see. As I walked from one building to the next, I noticed that I was in a very large glass room that was once beautiful. Hanging from the ceiling of this room were many plants that had not received care. The plants were wilted and had very little life left in them. If they weren't watered soon, they would surely die. I also noticed that the room was filled with nice, high-quality ping-pong tables that had obviously been in use. I could see that people had come here to play but didn't care at all about the plants.

Heading toward the back of the room, I noticed a hospital bed pushed to the side. In the bed there was indeed a woman. She was lying in a fetal position and looked close to death. I was going to pass by and ignore her as the man had told me to do, but I couldn't. I was compelled to come closer. The woman was hooked to an IV and had a podium over her bed. It was a fancy, clear Plexiglas podium. On top of the podium was a large Bible that was opened.

The woman called for me to come close to her. She had her checkbook out and wanted me to help her write a check to some anointed ministries that were serving the Lord. Immediately in my dream, I realized who this woman was and what was happening to her. She was the owner of the vast estate surrounding the gas station, and the people running the store were taking advantage of her. They were poisoning her and taking what was rightfully hers. The IV was part of the poison, but much of the poison was coming from those who were opening the Scriptures for her. Their words had put this woman in her sickened state. She was writing checks to anointed ministries when she was supposed to be doing anointed ministry.

God told me to prophesy to the woman. I began to shout, "Rise up, woman! Get out of your sickbed! Stop taking the medicines that are poisons to your system and listening to the words that are also poison to your soul. Get out of bed, and rule over your estate. You are not sick. God has made you well! The people you thought were caring for you were actually poisoning and robbing you. They want your money, and they want to rule over you. Stop it! Don't allow yourself to be taken advantage of anymore. Be strong, and rule over what God has given you. You don't need to send your money to someone else who has the anointing. Walk in your anointing!"

When I woke from that dream, at first I wondered if something I had eaten hadn't agreed with me! That was my rule of thumb with any wild dream. I had no clue what the dream meant, but there was no doubt in my mind that it had come from God.

As I began to get an interpretation from God, I realized that the woman was the true Bride of Christ, His Church. The glass room represented the buildings we typically associate with Church today. The ping-pong tables represented the games, gimmicks, and programs we use to keep people entertained. The nearly dead plants represented the Church's lack of spiritual growth and its desperate need for water before death consumed what little life was left.

The woman was being poisoned by God's Word being used falsely. She had been told that she could not run the estate and that she needed to depend on someone else's anointing. Others had taught her that she needed to send her money to them because of their anointing. She was locked in a room where the anointing wasn't allowed to operate.

The Bride of Christ today needs to get out of her sickbed, learn to walk in her anointing, and take possession of her inheritance. She was meant to rule over creation, not lie in her sickbed. Her healing was in her deliverance from the bondage of the lies she had been taught and from her dependence on the silly games.

God impresses me now to tell all who read this, stop! Don't just run around and give your money to this ministry and that, so that the anointing can go forth from them. The problem is not in supporting anointed ministries; we, as well as other ministries, need support from the Body of Christ. The problem is that God is calling you to walk in anointing also. He wants you to rise up! It's time to stop lying in a sickbed and to put on God's anointing and become His disciples. Stop playing the silly games of entertainment-driven church.

Stop listening to those who tickle itching ears! You've been duped by a church culture that keeps you from being everything God wants you to be. The modern church system keeps you running at a frantic pace, carrying out programs that are not making disciples. Captives are not finding freedom. The sick are not being healed. The hungry are not fed. The naked are not clothed, and the blind do not receive their sight.

Listen and obey the voice of the living God, and rule over the vast estate your Father has given you. He wants you to accept all of your inheritance, to take up all of His armor and crush the enemy. The Church has been sick and anemic too long. We have cowered in fear of our spiritual enemy. We don't do spiritual warfare because we fear getting beaten up.

You are the Church. It's time to get into God's Word and find out what it really says. It's time to live God's Word. Be honest with yourself, and admit it. You don't live what you read. Spiritually, you've been content with so little. Ask God to forgive you, fill you up, and free you up to serve Him.

Ask Jesus to teach and disciple you. Ask God to show you what He considers successful ministry. Ask for His ideas of what makes a successful Church. Study Jesus' ministry and the ministry of His disciples. Study about the authority God gave Jesus, which Jesus gives to those who follow Him. (Some passages to consider include: Matthew 10; Matthew 28:19-20; Mark 3:13-15; Mark 6:6-7; Mark 16:9-19; and Luke 9–10.)

If you will commit to taking off the glasses you use to look at the world and will commit to looking at God's Word and asking Him to disciple you, it will change your life. Be honest when you study. Don't allow you or anyone else to talk yourself out of the clear reading of God's Word. Nothing is more exciting than being a disciple of Jesus and nothing could be worse than to be like the Pharisees or Teachers of the Law who heard what Jesus said and watched what Jesus did while scheming ways to kill Him because He didn't fit their theology.

We would like to offer you help on this journey of being a biblical disciple through our website, www.operationlightforce.com, where you will find more extensive teaching on all of the topics you find in *The Jesus Training Manual.*

Study Questions

1. Read Paul's encounter with the Lord in Acts 9:1-19. What was the apostle Paul like before this event? What was he like after this encounter? (See Acts 19:11-12.)

_____

_____

_____

2. Have you ever had a personal transformation experience like Paul's or like Richard's where everything you believed was brought into question and you reexamined your belief system?

_____

_____

_____

3. Are you willing to examine your personal belief system in light of Scripture and be completely honest?

_____

_____

_____

4. What are some things that hinder people from truly allowing their personal belief structure to be examined and scrutinized?

_____

_____

_____

5. Has the Lord ever taken you through a desert-type experience to teach you? Has the Lord ever spoken to you through a dream? Write or share about what God taught you.

_____

_____

_____

6. Read the last five paragraphs of this chapter again. What will you do about this challenge?

_____

_____

_____

CHAPTER 8

Out of the Desert—The Birth of a Revolution

Along with the members of our Sunday night fellowship, we served throughout the city. We were part of every type of citywide outreach that existed. We poured ourselves into Restoration '98 and '99, which brought Tony Evans to Tampa, and sought to bring together African American churches with mostly white churches. We were at everything we could go to that had a vision for bringing revival to the city. God opened many doors for me to speak at all kinds of churches—black churches, all types of charismatic churches, Baptist churches, Methodist churches, Hispanic churches, Presbyterian churches, large churches, small churches, and more.

In not one of those churches was I able to find all the facets of discipleship God was teaching me, though I did find bits and pieces here and there. This is not meant as a slam or an indictment on any church. In fact, I was blessed to learn many different things at so many different churches.

I had never heard a message or had one class on healing in roughly 30 years of church attendance. So when I saw one church advertising a series on healing, I went. It was great teaching—very biblical—and after the series was finished, the pastor and I met. He loved the story of what God was doing in my life and had begun to contemplate how I could serve them. I too wondered if this would be a place to settle. But God clearly said He had more to teach me before I settled back into any ministry, and I told the pastor no.

I was pouring much of my energy into any aspect of ministry that was geared toward uniting the Body of Christ to change the city. There were many pastors meeting and praying together. One man, David Chew, was another unsung hero. He was serving the city for no pay. Many people speak of the need to unite the churches, but few invest the time, money, and energy needed to accomplish this task. David and his wife, Jinger, had been involved in successful ministry in the past and were now living by faith, trusting God for their resources and leading ministry to unite the city. On the other side of Tampa Bay was another unsung hero, Daniel Bernard. Daniel was the leader of Somebody Cares Tampa Bay, a ministry that was seeking to unite churches to reach the city.

Somebody Cares sponsored various visionary leaders to come to Tampa and speak to the churches about things like praying for your city, reaching the city, and servant evangelism. They had mobilized many churches to pray and fast for 40 days. Daniel had walked the entire perimeter of Hillsborough County, praying for its people. He was an incredible leader and an example to many.

In November 1999, another gifted servant of God, Jose, invited me to a lunch meeting in downtown Tampa, where a group of youth ministers were going to hear from a leader of Harvest Evangelism about a City Reaching School. At the meeting, Jack Lagatella of Harvest Evangelism challenged the group of 10 to 12 youth workers with the vision of mobilizing students to reach their campuses through "prayer evangelism." "Prayer evangelism," he said, "is talking to God about your friends before you talk to them about God." He told testimonies of great moves of God that had happened in other cities. He talked of students "prayer walking" their campuses, blessing their principals and teachers, and of how God had worked in many schools through the power of prayer and blessing.

I loved the vision Jack was sharing and told Jose to count me in. I wanted to serve in whatever way I was needed. The next week we met at Jose's home to discuss the direction we would take to mobilize the students of our county to reach their schools. In Jose's living room were about ten veteran youth workers with more than 100 years of combined experience. We had seen just about everything youth ministry had to offer and had never seen a campus reached for Christ. We knew it would take more than a conference with the best speakers. We already had some of the best concerts in the country nearly every week, and they weren't the answer.

One of the testimonies that stood out to several of us was that of a youth group in California that had fasted for 40 days. That sounded radical, and the stories of what happened with that group were exciting. But we felt that simply fasting for the schools wasn't enough. Isaiah 58 tells us that true fasting is about caring for people and their needs. So we wanted to include practical elements that would mobilize the students to get outside their comfort zones and serve others.

Robert Leatherwood, a highly respected youth minister in the area, had been applying the principles of servant evangelism with his youth ministry for several years with great success. He told of practical ways his students had reached out to others, such as giving away candy and writing encouraging notes. Robert told us that many unchurched and dechurched students were being reached using these methods.

So we wanted to combine prayer evangelism with servant evangelism, adding a new concept we had read about in Ed Silvoso's *That None Should Perish*, called "blessing evangelism." Blessing evangelism is speaking words of life and blessing. It's based on Jesus' commissioning of the 72 in Luke 10.5, where He told them to first speak peace when they entered a house. Too often we are prone to judge others and speak condemnation. Jesus would speak life and hope and blessing. Blessing evangelism is also based on Proverbs 18:21, which declares, *"Death and life are in the power of the tongue..."* (NASB). Our words have the power to bring life to a person's spirit and soul, or to bring condemnation and death.

The group decided that we should give the students daily assignments related to these principles and combine this with fasting so that the spiritual climate could be transformed throughout the city's schools.

The next question was what to call these 40 days of prayer, serving, and blessing. And what would we call the kick-off rally we were planning? Jeff Yale, a veteran youth worker, stood up and said in his booming voice, "This means war!" Everyone agreed. The 40 days would be called, "This Means War." We also decided that if you're going to have a war, you need a boot camp—and "Boot Camp" became the name of our rally.

Sometime during the discussion, I leaned over to a dear friend who had come with me to the meeting. "I'm about to invest a significant portion of my life in this," I whispered. It was apparent that everything God had been doing in my life had been for a purpose, and that in His timing, He was going to make clear what He wanted me to do. Now I knew that this 40-day thing, this Boot Camp, would somehow impact my life. I was willing to sweep the floor for Jose or run copies. God had taken all my pride. I just wanted to sell out and do whatever was asked to accomplish His vision and purposes.

I had never imagined the possibility of entire schools being transformed, and now it seemed like we were on the verge of watching it take place. Everyone was excited and committed to seeing the vision impact our city. Now for the laborious task of coming up with the 40 assignments, a logo, T-shirts, a band, and so on! Not only that, but the pastors who were behind the event were telling us there was no way we could get students to fast for 40 days. We hadn't even questioned it! Had we in our zeal set our sights too high? We took it back to some of the guys, and no one wanted to back away. The pastors and city leaders relented with skepticism and backed the rally and the 40 days.

I was in touch with Jose on a daily basis, asking what I could do to help. We had come up with a logo and some of the daily assignments and had discussed a variety of other components when on New Year's Day, Jose called and asked me to take over the leadership. At first I refused and told Jose he was the point man. He said that God wanted me to be the point person for this event. Then I suggested we do it together. Again he insisted that God had told him that I was to take the point on this event.

But Jose was "the man" in Tampa as far as I was concerned. He was my mentor among networking youth leaders. I had not led an event like this before. Jose promised to support and encourage me and help in any way he could. So with five weeks to go, a great idea, and very little else, I poured myself into finishing the 40-day assignments, working with Somebody Cares Tampa Bay to organize youth leaders across the entire Bay area, and helping to raise the money to pull off the event.

Robert Leatherwood was very helpful with ideas for daily assignments. Once we came up with the assignments, they were typed on the fronts and backs of three letter-sized sheets of paper. Simple packets were made up, providing the students with all the tools they needed. Bazooka bubble gum and Warhead and Atomic FireBall candies were counted out for everyone to give away. There were dog tags to be worn as witnessing tools—and note cards were included so that encouraging notes could be written to teachers, students, and principals. There were WWJD bracelets and more. Each item was a tool to be used in reaching out to others.

The day before the event, Jack Lagatella and Mike May from Harvest Evangelism flew in to town. Another speaker, Benjy McNaughton from Harvest, came in separately. Fear didn't come into the picture until I picked up the guys at the airport. I was sure we had made a mistake. These guys were ready for the funny farm! Jack Lagatella, whom I had met in November, was telling me that Mike May, his partner, had multiple personalities as Mike sat in the back of the car, fighting to stay awake. The two had spent the entire year traveling the world, and it was beginning to show. My fears, however, were allayed as I heard the passion of their hearts. Mike May came from Scotland, and when I shared my love for the movie *Braveheart,* Mike went into a William Wallace speech. It was decided that he would do this the next night at Boot Camp in full Scottish garb. We even procured an authentic sword and costume.

The night came for Boot Camp, and about 750 students arrived from all over the Bay area. The evening was powerful, and all of the students made commitments to do the 40 days of assignments and fasting. We made radio spots to announce the daily assignments for the students. Many youth groups were ordering more packets and assignments for their students. Within days, the number of students doing the 40 days had grown to 1,000.

Our first testimony came from a girl who spent the first day praying at the front door of her school and anointing it with oil. Another girl had come along and asked, "What are you doing?" She told the girl she was praying for the school. The second girl asked, "You don't believe in that stuff, do you?" The first girl replied, "I certainly do. My God answers prayer." The other girl rolled her eyes and walked off. On Wednesday morning, the second girl came up to the young revolutionary and got her attention. "I was thinking about what you said, and I decided to go with my mother to church last night. I became a Christian," she said.

Then testimonies came pouring in from the youth groups, about students and at least one teacher accepting Christ. A principal came to know Christ at one school, and an assistant principal was led to Christ at another. At least one youth ministry doubled in size. Robert Leatherwood had brought 35 students to Boot Camp and had purchased an extra 40 packets for the rest of his youth group and students from a club at school. His senior high youth ministry had been averaging 65 students before the 40 days. By the end, they were running around 100 and would plateau at 130 students.

It didn't take long to realize that something unique and powerful had transpired. During that first 40 days, leaders from two other cities had heard what God was doing in Tampa and wanted us to help them carry out a "40-Day Revolution" in their cities. A new ministry was being birthed.

The next city we were asked to come to and help birth a Revolution in was Orlando. By now we knew we were a fledgling organization, though the packaging wasn't together yet. What we had put together in Tampa had happened in only five weeks' time. Now we were being asked to help another city pull off an event. The leaders we were working with loved the concept but could tell we still had a way to go before we had our act together. As a result of their not believing we had it all together, they chose to use our material and concept but birthed their own ministry. Their expectation was that they were capable of producing something superior to our material.

That was a painful experience. We thought that what God had led us to do was going to be jeopardized—and that even as we were being birthed, we would be overrun by the first city we helped to launch a Revolution. God gave us peace, however, assuring us that what He was going to do through our ministry and lives was only beginning, and that He was teaching us a lesson. We had no idea how far He was going to take us, or how much blessing He would pour in our laps in just a short amount of time.

In the second city where we helped to launch a Revolution, God led me to two men whom He used to mentor, encourage, and strengthen me. The host church and sponsor of the 40-Day Revolution in that city was First Assembly of God in Deland. Mike Modica and Mike Carroll were the pastor and associate pastor there.

These two men had given their lives to pastoring their entire city. Their church ministered to other churches. In a city of just 13,000, they had managed to build a monthly network of 35 to 50 pastors. These men had pledged their lives to one another, and each of them had come to have a citywide vision.

At their Boot Camp, they hosted more than 500 students at the local high school. When I had originally been called about bringing a Revolution to Deland, Mike Carroll told me that the principal was against Christians doing anything in the schools. Mike was close to calling the American Center for Law and Justice (ACLJ) so that the students' rights could be restored. The same principal had read through the 40-Day material and decided that there was nothing the students would be doing that he couldn't allow, so he opened the school to be rented. He warned that if anything got out of line, he would stop the whole thing.

After Boot Camp, the students began to evangelize with great zeal. One girl was used of God to lead 23 students to Christ during the first 20 days. One principal received a stack of more than 50 note cards from students, letting him know they appreciated him and were praying for him. There were stories of teachers crying over the note cards that had encouraged them. Youth groups experienced growth, and the whole city was impacted.

At the end of the school year, Deland did the 40-Day Revolution again with great impact. This time, men from many churches fasted for the students during the 40 days prior to Boot Camp. The results again were astounding. Even the principal who had been reluctant to allow Christians to do anything on his campus told Mike Carroll that the school had experienced only one fight and one drug incident all year. He attributed this to the students who had been taking part in the Revolution. He told Mike that anything he wanted to do on the campus was fine with him. If they wanted an entire school assembly, all they had to do was ask. Mike ran to get his planner so the opportunity wouldn't slip away. Mike was able to book an entire school assembly the following fall, with Reggie Dabbs, a powerful youth evangelist, as the speaker.

One powerful story that illustrates what happens during the 40-Day Revolution occurred with a few church kids who took the challenge to heart and were used by God. During Boot Camp, several students caught a passion to reach out through serving, blessing, and praying for a group of Goth students at their school. They realized that they had always judged these students and condemned them; now they wanted to show them the love of God.

The students began to pray every day for the seven Goth students on their campus. They soon overcame the intimidation factor and began to serve them and write them encouraging notes. On days like "Donut Day," they made sure that the Goths got donuts. Every day they prayed for them, served them, and spoke words of encouragement and life. During the 40 days, one of the leaders of the group became a Christian. Without anyone preaching to him, this student had such a radical change that he decided to get rid of his Gothic clothing. He said that his clothes had represented the pain and darkness in his heart and that Christ had filled his heart with light. By the end of the 40 days, six of the seven Goths had chosen to make Jesus the Lord of their lives. No one had set out to change the way they dressed or wore their hair. Christian students had simply loved them and shown them what Jesus would do if they met Him. The impact of a few revolutionary students had transformed the schools of another city.

Because of the testimonies from these few Revolutions, others began to line up, and a large denomination chose to host us for their spring convention and launch a Revolution statewide. By the next spring there were 4,000 students doing the 40-Day Revolution at one time, and more than 6,000 completed the 40 days during the first year.

Harvest Evangelism was so excited that they wanted to host a youth leaders' meeting in San Jose to share about the 40-Day Revolution. Only two weeks before the meeting, Harvest called and said that the agenda had changed. This was very disappointing since I had already bought tickets to California, but I trusted that God was ultimately in control. We hadn't sought such an honor and weren't going to complain when it was taken away. They were now going to promote another initiative that had come out of California, called The Call DC.

The Call DC was the brainchild of a California youth pastor who had a vision of a million teenagers coming to Washington DC in September 2000. My first thought was that there was no way this was going to happen. I had never heard of The Call. I figured this youth pastor from California was on some kind of an ego trip.

When I arrived in San Jose and made my way to the conference, I was surprised to see a couple I knew from St. Petersburg. As I was walking up to them, I overheard them telling a man about a guy in Tampa who was calling students to do a 40-day fast. I spoke up and said, "I know that guy!" Surprised to see me, they quickly introduced me to Lou Engle, the California youth pastor who was the visionary behind The Call. Lou and I chatted for a few minutes, and there was an immediate connection in our spirits.

As the conference was about to begin, Lou asked if I had a card. I didn't, but I had just gotten five copies of the newest edition of *The 40-Day Revolution*. I handed a copy to Lou, and he handed me a copy of his book, *Fast Forward*. As the conference began, I thumbed through Lou's book, realizing that he, too, was calling the youth of the nation to a 40-day fast. I saw that one of the illustrations in his book was nearly word-for-word the same as an illustration I had used. There was no doubt about it. God was doing something incredible! God had put in the hearts of two people from opposite ends of the nation the very same passion.

I looked across the room to where Lou was sitting. He had been looking through my book, *The 40-Day Revolution*. He too had thumbed through the pages and realized that God was doing something incredible. We both just about came out of our seats! The only problem was, everyone else was listening intently to some powerful teaching from Ed Silvoso. As soon as the teaching was done, Lou and I connected. He told me then and there that he wanted to be able to use our material at The Call DC. He wanted a million copies by September! I was stunned. My faith had grown a lot over the last few years, but that was like raising the dead kind of faith, and I wasn't there yet.

Lou and I began to have regular contact, and he would always say that he wanted a million copies for The Call DC. My concern was, *Where was I going to get the money?* The event was free. Every organization was giving away its material. I was living by faith and had no money. This task seemed as enormous as picking up Mount Everest and dropping it in the ocean.

One day I was sharing about our ministry with a business owner who had chosen to support it. As a side note, I told him about The Call. He told me to call them that day and tell them that if they were serious, we'd have the books there. I was stunned again. I had written this off as impossible, and here I was being told that the mountain was on its way into the ocean. I heard the Lord speak to me, "O ye of little faith."

In the end, we did give away 30,000 copies at The Call, where somewhere between 350,000 and 450,000 believers gathered for a day of fasting and prayer. We gave away every last copy we had and didn't expect the immediate response we received. As we were driving home the next day, one of my board members called and told me that our phone message recorder was full and that we needed to clear it so people could leave messages. That seemed odd. We called right away to retrieve our messages and already had orders for hundreds more books. In the next three weeks we sold close to 8,000 more books. Many downloaded free copies of *The 40-Day Revolution* from the Internet. Somewhere in the neighborhood of 40,000 to 50,000 students were engaged in a Revolution. At The Call, all 350,000 had committed to doing the Revolution, but most didn't know what it was or where to get it. Who knows how many really did get copies off the website! Our little website got 25,000 hits that month. Requests came in from all over the country, and we were soon booking events as far away as Salt Lake City.

In one year, God had taken the Revolution from a very humble beginning to a national platform. We soon realized we were not at all ready for all that God had given and that He was still building a foundation. In the midst of birthing this ministry, God was still in the process of discipling us and teaching us more about His Kingdom.

Today Operation Light Force continues to mobilize believers all around the world to carry out 40-day strategies of prayer and fasting, serving and blessing, and sharing the faith. We have expanded to include an adult version, a children's version, and a college version. Entire churches and cities take part in this strategy with the vision of bringing about transformation and revolution in their regions.

We continue to hear incredible testimonies of how God has used people to reach others during these 40-day campaigns. The book *The 40-Day Revolution,* published by NavPress, has been translated into Korean, Spanish, and Portuguese.

It's amazing what God can do with a life when the individual begins to listen to Him. I believe that God has a much bigger vision for our lives, if we would only listen to Him and obey Him. Don't be surprised at what God will do if you get outside of your box and let Him be all He wants to be in your life. The ride has been so exciting thus far. I can't wait to see what God has around the next corner.

For many people, the great fear is letting God have complete control. They ask themselves, "What will God do if I give Him my life? He'll probably send me to live in a hut in Africa." Maybe. God has the right to ask anything of us and expect obedience. Yet our Father loves us, and I believe that in surrendering to Him, we find out what life more abundant really can be.

Today the Revolution lives on through the ministry of Operation Transformation and you can find out more at www.operationtransformation.com. There are resources for every age group that will radically transform you, your church, your school, your workplace, your city, and even a nation.

Study Questions

1. What is God doing in your city to bring about a transformation and a revolution of change? How are you involved?

   _____

   _____

   _____

2. What in your city needs to be transformed? Take some time right now to pray for those areas that you need to see God do a miracle.

   _____

   _____

   _____

3. What are some instances that you can remember from God's Word where, after taking someone through a desert experience, God used him or her in a more powerful way? (Hint: Joseph, Elijah, Jesus, Moses, etc.)

   _____

   _____

   _____

4. What would happen in your city if 100, 500, 1,000 or more believers decided to fast for 40 days and would pray for their coworkers, fellow students, neighbors, friends, and enemies?

   _____

   _____

   _____

5. What can God do if you give Him your life? What holds people back
   from full surrender to His will? What blessings could we be missing?

   _____

   _____

   _____

CHAPTER 9

A Year of Breakthroughs

As the new ministry was developing, the Lord continued to disciple our small group, which gathered on Sunday nights for worship and study—and on Friday nights, when we focused on intense prayer for the city. It's hard to put into words what took place in those days and all that the Spirit of God was teaching us. Our only text for study was the Word of God, and we began to explore truths of God's Word that had been neglected by our church traditions. We examined healing, how God speaks, visions, dreams, faith, miracles, the Kingdom of God, casting out evil spirits, and more.

When you're studying healing and a sick person comes along, you tend to have greater faith and figure, *What have I got to lose? Let's pray for this person and see what God does!* You also begin to learn truths from God's Word that make your praying more effective and powerful. We began to see people healed on a fairly consistent basis. One night as we were listening to the testimony of a man God had used to heal others, a woman in the group told us she'd been diagnosed with cancer and would be going in for surgery. I prayed over her with greater faith than I'd ever had before. She said she knew God healed her cancer that night.

Later that week, we received a call from our friend, and she was ecstatic. Not only was the cancer healed, but the doctors were shocked by another miracle. At first they wanted to do her blood work again. They were certain that somehow her blood sample had gotten mixed up with another's. When the results came back the second time, the doctors told her the results had them baffled. You see, this friend had lived a hard life. Once she had been a prostitute, a drug user, and homeless. To look at her now, you'd never guess it. But during that time, she had contracted hepatitis A, B, and C. Now the doctors were saying these were gone!

During this period, a Baptist pastor named Len Harper and I became close friends. We played tennis or basketball together on a weekly basis. After a game, he'd pick my brain for hours about what God was teaching me. He couldn't believe all that was happening in my life. He'd debate different facets of what I was saying, and it helped sharpen my mind and strengthen my beliefs. He wrestled with how I could minister to Christians who had evil spirits tormenting them. He believed in healing but had no experience in it. I shared all that God was teaching me and the miracles I was beginning to see Him do in my life. Len couldn't always accept what I said, but he knew I wasn't lying.

This friendship had a healing effect on me. It felt like all of my close friends in ministry had rejected me and what God was doing in my life. I was experiencing the most exciting, amazing time of my life and ministry, yet the very people I had loved and respected most wrote me off and closed the doors of ministry from me. The fact that this one Baptist preacher would listen to me was a great encouragement. I had felt the sting of rejection from the church, and since the most natural response when rejected is to return the rejection, I struggled with the temptation to reject the church as I then knew it.

To this point, most of our ministry had been to people who were relatively unknown, and though they had experienced miraculous breakthroughs and deliverance, the word of what God was doing spread slowly. The people we ministered to discovered that when they shared about how they'd been set free from strongholds, people usually expressed indifference or unbelief. Many times the things God had delivered them from were not what you'd want to put in the headlines anyway. There are many amazing stories of God's miraculous power setting people free or healing people that I cannot write about because many people don't want their story told. We honor that.

As my relationship grew with Len and his wife, Robin, I realized that there were many areas of life where God could work to set them free. We had begun to swap baby-sitting services with the Harpers, and when I was in their beautiful home, I noticed a high level of spiritual turmoil. The children went to bed every night with the lights on. One child woke up nearly every night with night terrors—an experience far more terrifying than a regular nightmare. A child who has night terrors typically gets out of bed and has violent reactions to what he saw in the dream, yet many times does not remember the tormenting dream.

As I baby-sat the children, I began to take the spiritual authority God had been teaching me about, to break the power of the enemy. Len and Robin often came home to find me worshiping or praying around their house. They noticed that on the nights when I watched their children, their son didn't have night terrors.

Robin began to ask questions. Whenever we baby-sat, Robin had a list of questions that took us an hour or more to process. When it was just Robin, Dawn, and I, she would open up even more. Robin was greatly embarrassed to ask us questions about the things she was experiencing. For a long time, she had been seeing a psychological therapist and was on medication for depression. For years she had been seeing things in her home. She hadn't even told her therapist these things because she feared she'd be locked away. I told her we had ministered to many people who told of hearing voices, seeing loved ones who had already died, encountering evil spirits, and much more. Most of the people who shared these encounters said the same thing: they told no one about their experiences because they thought people would think they were crazy.

Robin had to enter the hospital for six weeks because the torment was so great and all the medicines weren't helping. Now she was in the same troubled state that had sent her to the hospital for help in the past. Robin borrowed a book from us, *Healing Through Deliverance* by Peter Horrobin—one of the best and most thoroughly biblical books I have found on this subject. Reading Horrobin's book, Robin began to have hope that her torment might have an end. At the same time she was gripped with a fear that caused her to want to run away from that hope. Finally, Robin decided that the pain of not getting help was greater than the fear of what could happen.

Robin was in very bad shape when she came to meet with me and another friend, Nicole Leu. In fact, she couldn't even walk from her van to the house where we were meeting. As we sat down with Robin, God filled me with great faith that He was going to set her free. I knew Robin was ready; she wanted to be free. I told Robin she would be free of fear and torment before she left the room—and filled with joy and peace. Robin looked at me as if I were some salesman making an impossible promise. "I know you don't believe me now," I said, "but you'll see!"

Two hours later, Robin was laughing, smiling, and shaking her head in disbelief. I teased, "You didn't believe me, did you?" Robin said there was no way she'd have believed it was possible.

For a month, Robin experienced freedom, joy, and a peace she had never known before. Len said it was like being married to a totally different person. When Robin, Len, and the kids went away on vacation to see Robin's family, all of the torment came back. There were ungodly soul ties we had not broken during the first meeting. *Ungodly soul ties* is a term that refers to relationships that hold a controlling influence in a person's life. Many times those people are no longer a part of someone's life, but the experiences that a person had with him or her still control the way one thinks or acts. In Robin's case, there were many people who had hurt her or taken advantage of her. Those wounds still affected the way she viewed herself, men, and even her own husband.

When Len and Robin returned, I sent Robin to some friends who run a ministry called New Beginnings. They had been ministering deliverance for 15 years and were able to discern some things I hadn't dealt with. It was good for me to watch and learn from their experience. Today, Robin has been free from the things that tormented her for years. She now has a growing ministry of speaking at churches and teaching believers how to minister freedom to others. Her testimony has caused the rapid expansion of this type of ministry and given it greater legitimacy in the minds of many. People can see the transformation in Robin.

For example, a woman named Laura began coming to our Sunday night home church, and Robin's testimony and ministry of deliverance soon touched her world in an amazing way. We had known Laura at another church several years before, and in the meantime, her husband had left her. Laura told us all about the hardships she and her children were experiencing. It was heartbreaking, and we asked God how we could minister to Laura. She had only been coming about three weeks when we began to study the power of God to answer prayer.

This particular night we were looking at the necessity of faith in prayer. James 5:15 says, *"And the prayer offered in faith will make the sick person well; the Lord will raise him up. If he has sinned, he will be forgiven."* The way we pray does make a difference, and I had never been part of a prayer group that knew how to pray the faith-filled prayers that produce results. If I were to give you an exhaustive list of Scriptures pertaining to God answering prayer and faith in prayer, it would fill another book! God's promises of answered prayer, examples of answered prayer, and the correlation between faith and prayer are replete in Scripture.

Most of our Christian lives, Dawn and I had approached prayer as a valuable exercise where we asked God to do whatever He wanted to do. We had always heard that it was presumptuous to pray anything but "God, if it's Your will…." The funny thing is, nowhere in the Bible do we see anyone pray, "If it be Your will." Even Jesus, when asking for the cup of suffering to be removed from Him, said, *"My Father, if it is not possible for this cup to be taken away unless I drink it, may Your will be done"* (Matt. 26:42). Jesus knew what His Father's will was and wanted it to be accomplished. Yet He had a human side that dreaded the cross. What we see is the torment between what Jesus, the man, wanted and what He knew to be God's will. If anything, we need to be willing to admit that much of what we ask for is according to the human will, not the will of God.

Our study group was learning that God wanted us to stand upon the truths in His Word and ask with faith for things that are in accordance with His will. God had taught us many keys to praying and seeing answers to prayer, so at the end of our study, we asked Laura what she wanted God to do and what she would be willing to believe God for. She said she wanted her marriage restored. Victor had told her that the Lord or an angel would have to come and tell him to reconcile before he would consider it. Against all odds, we prayed, and God filled me with assurance that He was going to answer our prayers. I told Laura that she was going to receive what she asked for and that it was going to come quickly. Laura would surely know that the power of God had done this!

I had to urge Laura not to take what I was saying lightly. It was more than positive thinking. I wanted her to remember my words so that she would know it wasn't just good luck but an answer to prayer. Though I knew God had heard us, I also sensed that we were to fast as a group for seven days to seal this prayer. Each couple in the group chose a day to fast for Victor and Laura.

On Wednesday of the same week, I was going to hear Robin give her testimony for the first time at her church. After a time of worship, Len told the church how God had transformed Robin and that it was like being married to a different woman. He said that the past few months had been the best in their marriage, and he expressed that this type of ministry was going to become a normal part of their Baptist church.

Robin came forward to share how Christ had healed her depression, delivered her from all the medication she'd been taking, and removed the torment that had filled her soul for as long as she could remember.

In walked Victor, and my jaw almost hit the floor! He'd been living in Orlando, which is over an hour away. That afternoon he had called Len to talk about what was happening in his life. Len had been looking for Victor's phone number so he could invite him to hear Robin. Figuring it couldn't hurt, Victor had come. I had to leave early and never got to talk to Victor that night, but I knew he would be impacted by Robin's testimony. I prayed that Victor would be open to the idea of deliverance.

On Sunday night when we got with our small group, Laura looked distraught. She had gotten an e-mail from Victor, explaining that he had gone through deliverance and was a new person. He told her his life had been totally transformed. He said he wasn't sure whether it would make a difference in their marriage, but he wanted Laura to go through this ministry as well. He even thought it would be good for their children.

Laura was concerned. Was this of God, or was Victor involved in some kind of cult? It's amazing how many people assume deliverance is cultic when it was part of Jesus' Discipleship 101 training! I assured Laura of the biblical basis for what Victor had gone through and told her what had happened to Robin. Laura hadn't known that Victor was present when Robin gave her testimony. She decided she would be willing to receive deliverance ministry as well.

Within two weeks, Victor and Laura were sitting in our small group, smiling. God had healed their marriage and set both of them free from spiritual and emotional strongholds. Victor had been building a relationship with another woman (because he had been certain their marriage was over), and that relationship was totally broken off as well. Because soul ties had been broken during the deliverance, all of Victor's desire for the other woman—which had been very strong—was now broken. He could see that the very relationship he had thought would become his "next step" had really been a part of satan's trap.

Breakthroughs like this seem rare in traditional counseling sessions because counseling deals with the mind, will, and emotions. Deliverance ministry deals not only with the soul of a person but also his or her spirit and any spirits that have been given a place in that person's life. We invite spirits of darkness to torment us by opening the doors to our souls. We do this by harboring unforgiveness, through sexual relationships, the occult, drugs, by exposing ourselves to ungodly influences like pornography, violence, and murder, and in many other ways.

With the strongholds broken and a newfound freedom, Victor gained a new passion in his heart and a new vision. Over the next eight months, he earned a master's degree in biblical marriage and family counseling, and his marriage to Laura became a source of joy. His life has been transformed.

Laura's prayers were answered, and it shows on her face. She is filled with joy and gladness at the awesome power of God. Our whole group watched the incredible process and learned more about God's grace and power. All the members of our group have since opened up to deliverance ministry and have been set free from fear and torment that had come into their lives through sexual abuse, depression, verbal abuse, sin, and a host of other ways. All of them have begun to exercise more of the authority and power that is available to them through Christ, by His resurrection power. Most have been used by God to pray for the sick or those in spiritual bondage. The fruits that resulted from Jesus' teaching of the 12 and the 72 in Luke 10 were born in the lives of our small group.

In Len and Robin's church, a new training ministry was birthed. In just one year, more than a hundred individuals and families went through ministry to experience freedom and victory. God has transformed their church, their family, and every facet of their lives. Their children now sleep through the night without the torment of nightmares. The church is experiencing growth and blessing beyond anything they've experienced before.

One night when Len and I were playing tennis, we saw another pastor, Steve Minter, and his son playing on another court. Len and I made our way over to ask them to play doubles, and as we chatted, Steve shared about being very discouraged.

After the game, Steve opened up even more. He told us that he'd been battling depression for several years and was so discouraged that he wanted to quit. He then told us about his problem with rage. As a pastor, he felt like a failure. How could he offer hope to anyone when he was so miserable himself? His life at home with his wife and children was not what it should have been.

Steve was as desperate as he had ever been. He was crying out for help. Len began to explain about the transformation Robin had experienced. He shared how she was thoroughly delivered from depression and had even stopped taking medication. Steve had graduated from Dallas Theological Seminary and was a serious Bible teacher. In his heart, he had wondered if what he was battling was demonic, but his theological framework allowed no understanding of how to deal with this type of spiritual battle. All his Bible reading and prayer hadn't made a dent in the core issues he was dealing with.

Steve had recently read Jack Deere's *Surprised by the Spirit*. Having sat under Jack's teaching in seminary, he was challenged by the book and by the concept of a God who still moves in power today. Steve went to one of Jack Deere's conferences and had wanted God to touch and heal him of his battles with rage, depression, and sexual temptation. God touched Steve in a powerful way that night, and he found freedom and relief in these areas. But within a few weeks, he began to struggle again with the same problems.

Robin's testimony gave a glimmer of hope to Steve. He was desperate enough to try anything. Before opening himself up to deliverance ministry, Steve thoroughly investigated what was being taught at Len and Robin's church. Because of the incredible transformation they had experienced, Robin had begun a monthly Freedom Conference at the church. In this course, she taught the basics of how people open the door to demonic strongholds. She taught on how to break curses and be free from strongholds that are passed on from generation to generation in families. Her four-hour training and the homework that accompanied it were not only biblical, but also made practical sense and shed light on what was happening to Steve.

Steve submitted to ministry, and the impact was immediate. The uncontrollable rage and depression were gone. Steve's faith in the power of God was transformed. Steve began to apply what he had been taught to his own family and household. Again, the results were amazing! One day Steve's son came under severe attack. The symptoms were physical, but Steve discerned that the issue was really spiritual. Steve addressed the strongholds in his son's life and asked him to repent. Steve then took this newfound authority, which had been his all along, and applied it to his son's life. His son experienced freedom and healing then and there!

A new chapter was being written in Steve's life. He began to realize that throughout his congregation there were people with strongholds that all the counseling in the world couldn't fix. He began to see that the key issues were deeper than the intellects of these people. As much as they needed sound biblical teaching, they first needed to experience freedom from the things that bound them. This way, they would be able to receive the truth.

Steve began to seek out solid teaching about how to set people free. He thoroughly digested *Healing Through Deliverance* by Peter Horrobin and other books on the subject. Using some of Robin's material and supplementing it with other truths he had researched, Steve developed a training manual and began to take his church down the road to freedom. In his first class, 45 people were taught, and 15 of them came back on Saturday for ministry. Now Steve's training is a regular part of the ministry at his church. In fact, its impact has transformed the church!

This is just a small sampling of the lives that have been impacted in this way. Every month, anywhere from 15 to 45 people are going through this ministry. One Christian counselor in town experienced healing when we prayed for her, and she began bringing her clients to us for ministry. Many had been from counselor to counselor, yet the power of God healed and set them free in a matter of hours. This counselor's own ministry has been transformed. She is now a part of our ministry team and says there is no comparison between the results she used to experience and what she now sees in life transformation through healing and deliverance ministry.

We are seeing teenagers getting free. Many pastors from Brandon and the surrounding region have received ministry and freedom. Numerous marriages that seemed hopelessly on the brink of destruction have been restored. The power of God is being restored to His Church.

In one year, the power of God literally transformed the lives of hundreds in the Brandon, Florida area. Churches that were once filled with Christians who sat Sunday after Sunday with their nice clothes, pretty smiles, and empty hearts are now finding the joy that comes when the power of God sets them free from the secret things that bring torment. They are learning the keys to keeping that freedom and how to help others find release from bondage in Christ.

We are seeing biblical discipleship restored to the Church. Believers and church leaders are beginning to study and understand more about the Kingdom of God as Jesus preached it, as well as about Jesus' ministry of equipping His disciples to cast out evils spirits and heal the sick. In Revelation 12:10-11 we read:

> *Now have come the salvation and the power and the kingdom of our God, and the authority of His Christ. For the accuser of our brothers, who accuses them before our God day and night, has been hurled down. They overcame him by the blood of the Lamb and by the word of their testimony; they did not love their lives so much as to shrink from death.*

We have been given the hope of salvation. God's power is available for us today. Jesus told us that the Kingdom of God has come. God has given us more authority than we know what to do with. He restored our authority through the cross. Satan's authority has been compromised because of the blood of Jesus. We must learn to operate in our authority and overcome satan's schemes. You have read the testimonies of just a few of those God has set free, and God will use these testimonies even in your heart as He has used them in the hearts of many.

Has something in the stories I've shared struck a chord with you? Is your marriage in serious trouble? You may have been to counselors, but for some reason the person you once couldn't live without seems a million miles away. Maybe you're battling overwhelming depression, on medications that keep you drugged up, and unable to truly experience life.

Could there be more?

God wants to offer you freedom. God is more powerful than any drug you can take. He is wiser than the best counselor money can afford. Even Christian counselors may be trying to deal with your soul (mind, will, and emotions) when the problem is spiritual.

Many object at this point, saying, "You can't blame the devil for all your problems." The devil isn't to blame. He's doing what he does best. We are responsible to some degree when anything demonic gains a foothold in our lives. We can overcome, but not unless someone shows us how.

Others say, "You believe there's a demon behind every bush!" The truth is, they're not hiding in the bushes! Today the demonic parades and flaunts itself everywhere you look. Just because we can't see the invisible realm of the spirit doesn't make it any less real. We are assaulted with opportunities to sin and open the door to strongholds. Sexuality is thrown in our faces—from the magazine racks in grocery stores to the Internet and TV, and even in public places. The occult is being thrown at us with unprecedented force. Most books, movies, video games, and other media forms are full of it, and we think it's only a game. Need I continue? Opportunities to develop strongholds have hounded us since the day we were born, and most would admit that at some point we compromised with sin. Today we may feel powerless to overcome the strongholds that sin left in our lives.

I would encourage you to be open to the ministry of freedom through deliverance. Just as in any area of ministry, there are those who are wise and mature and those who would minister outside the bounds of Scripture. One way to discern whether someone is effective and biblical in their approach to freedom-type ministry is to ask yourself the question, "Do you see lasting fruit in the lives of people who are ministered to?" It is also critical to ask God to give you discernment. God wants to set you free! God has been equipping an army of disciples all over the world. You should be able to find someone who can minister to you. Don't give up. You can be free. We offer various forms of ministry at Operation Light Force. We offer weekly ministry from trained ministers or a five-day intensive where significant healing and breakthrough take place in people's lives. Our online resources have also been effective in people's lives to help them find freedom and healing.

One woman e-mailed us that she had been healed of bi-polar, schizophrenia, Post Traumatic Stress Disorder, and been able to come off all of her 11 medications after one month on our website and diligently working through our courses. She ended up coming for an intensive and then came to work at our ministry for a while. Today she is ministering back in her home town. Maybe one day that will be your story.

Study Questions

1. Which of the stories/testimonies in this chapter impacted you the most, and why?

_____

_____

_____

2. Have you seen Christian leaders in your city who are in bondage to strongholds whose lives and ministries would be transformed and healed by the power of God? How would it impact your city to see their lives transformed?

_____

_____

_____

3. Does the Bible teach us to pray for the sick by saying "if it is your will"? Did Jesus or the disciples pray that way? Did anyone in Scripture? Why do we pray that way?

_____

_____

_____

4. How tragic would it be for someone to live his or her entire Christian life with the power of God so available for him or her to find freedom and to set others free and yet never to experience that freedom or minister that freedom to others?

_____

_____

_____

5. What are you going to do to begin to see lasting fruit in your own life and in the lives of the people you minister to?

_____

_____

_____

CHAPTER 10

Hearing the Voice of God

From the beginning of God's Word, we see God creating man and fellowshipping with him (see Gen. 2). God spoke to Adam and Eve. He even walked with them in the Garden of Eden (see Gen. 3:8). Adam and Eve hid from God when they sinned, and thus began the breakdown in communication between mankind and God.

Even after the fall of man, God continued to speak to men and women. In Genesis 4, we see God speaking to Cain and Abel. In Genesis 5, we see Enoch walking with God. Whether Enoch's walk with God was literally in the flesh or spiritually, as you or I would walk with Him today, we are not certain. However, the writer of Hebrews tells us that Enoch never saw death. He was taken up to Heaven to be with God (see Heb. 11:5).

The Lord also spoke to Noah, Abraham, Isaac, and Jacob. God even sent an angel to speak to Hagar (see Gen. 16:11-12). God spoke to Sarah, and He spoke to Joseph. All of the principal people in Genesis heard God speak to them in one form or another. God spoke through visions, dreams, and in person, and always very specifically. We don't always know that God spoke audibly, but we never find a reference to an impression from God—a "maybe God said." The words God spoke to His people were recorded for us, and for centuries believers have trusted that these are indeed the words God spoke.

God spoke to Moses in many ways and more than 150 times. In Numbers 7:89, we find God speaking to Moses in an audible voice. Normally it is not stated specifically that God spoke in an audible voice, so when we read about God speaking we can't be sure whether it refers to an audible voice, the quiet voice in one's spirit, or some other form of communication.

Throughout the Word, we see a God who is actively engaged with His people. I searched the Scriptures to find out how common it was for God to speak to men and women. In fact, I am working on a study Bible and a book about God speaking. It began while researching God speaking in Scripture. I started copying and pasting passages where God was speaking, and I realized quickly that I may as well copy the entire Bible.

Is God in the business of speaking? Did He decide at some point that He was tired of communicating directly, and did He send us His manual to follow instead? Here are just some of the ways that Scripture tells of God communicating with His people.

- "God spoke"—13
- "God said"—44
- "The Lord spoke"—138
- Variations of "the Lord said"—326
- Revealed/revelation—99
- Dreams—93
- Visions—100

That's a total of 813 passages in which God spoke to His people, and there are so many more. To put it in perspective, I found 503 references to Heaven and 156 mentions of salvation in the Bible. Few people who love God and believe the Bible would tell you there's no Heaven or that salvation is not for today. Yet I'm amazed at how many believers will say they've never heard God speak to them. These people are often frustrated, hurt, and even angry that someone would suggest that we can hear God speak today.

Many evangelicals teach that God no longer speaks except through Scripture. Some wrongly base it on the teaching of Martin Luther called *sola scriptura*. These teachers contend that if you want to know what God has to say, Scripture is the only reliable source. Yet the truth is, God speaks today in all of the ways He has used since the beginning of time. Scripture is the measuring stick by which we judge any revelation from God. God will not say something today that contradicts what is in His Word. Scripture should be the root of all Christian teaching. It is not the only way that God speaks to us. If what you think God is telling you doesn't line up with Scripture, then you are in trouble.

One profound reference to how God speaks is found in John 10. First we see that it was God who spoke these words. Jesus was God in the flesh. He was "the Word," in living color for all to see. He embodied what a disciple was to say, be, and do.

In John 10, Jesus tells us that His sheep hear His voice and will listen to no other. Jesus says that the reason we follow Him is because we know His voice. Do you know the voice of God? I believe God speaks to all of us throughout our lives. He desires an intimate relationship with every believer. The problem is that we have allowed our sins to separate us from God. We haven't learned to discern God's voice as opposed to the many other voices in the world.

Television communicates its philosophy, morality, and vision to us. Today's school systems have a clearly defined will for our lives and are adept at communicating their ideals. The world's philosophy is spoken to us, sung to us, and written in thousands of publications. No one would deny that the world speaks to us in a myriad of ways. Yet many struggle to believe that God speaks today in the many ways He did in Scripture. I've even had both Christians and Jehovah's Witnesses tell me that the devil can speak to us but God doesn't. Wow, how does that line up? The devil can speak but your God cannot. What kind of religion is that? A dead one that doesn't line up with God's Word.

Jesus taught us an important lesson about His own ministry. In John 5:19, Jesus said that even He could do nothing except what He saw the Father doing:

> *Then Jesus answered and said to them, "Most assuredly, I say to you, the Son can do nothing of Himself, but what He sees the Father do; for whatever He does, the Son also does in like manner"* (NKJV).

The practical way we see this in operation is by looking at how Jesus ministered to others. Studying Jesus' healing ministry can be very frustrating. He doesn't give a step-by-step process to follow. It's not like you can find one way to heal blindness, another formula for leprosy, and another three easy steps for raising the dead or helping the lame walk. Why is that? Sure, Jesus sent the 12 and the 72 out in Luke 9 and 10, but what did they say when they encountered a demon or someone with leprosy? We need to know so we can copy them. Right?

Don't you wish it were that simple? What you learn from a study of Jesus' ministry is that He and His disciples had to learn to hear the voice of God. Since Jesus never handled a problem the same way twice, how else would the disciples have learned what to do?

Hearing God's voice is fundamental to being a disciple and a Christian. The reason Jesus doesn't say in John 10 that His sheep need to learn to listen to His voice is that it's a given! There are many things in Scripture that are simply assumed. The reason Scripture fails to address some topics is that many truths we wrestle with today were simply known to be true. People weren't hung up on whether God spoke; they just listened and responded. People in the early Church didn't question the reality of the demonic as we do. They knew for sure the things we often debate. Read that last sentence again.

You can't be an effective disciple if you don't learn to listen to God's voice. Jesus makes clear that there are other voices, but He says that His sheep will not listen to them. Now that I know the voice of God, when people try to reason with me that God doesn't speak, I have very little patience. Almost daily God tells me very specific things about people and situations. He has told me the name of one pastor's first girlfriend, the demonic books that a certain girl was reading, specific details about someone's abuse, and even things that will happen in the future. I don't have any special gift that sets me apart. I simply began to ask God to teach me how to hear His voice. He did, and it's incredible. You can too. This is one of my favorite things to teach people, and at conferences it is a favorite.

Jesus warned in the Gospels that a day would come when believers would be persecuted because of our faith in Him. He said we would be arrested but that we shouldn't worry about what we would say. Jesus promises us that we will not be the ones doing the talking, but it will be "the Spirit of your Father speaking through you." (See Matthew 10:17-20; Mark 13:11-13; and Luke 21:12-17.)

In Matthew 10, Jesus tells us that He will reveal secrets to us and says, *"What I tell you in the dark, speak in the daylight; what is whispered in your ear, proclaim from the roofs"* (Matt. 10:27). Until I learned to pay attention to the voice of the Holy Spirit, I missed out on so much valuable ministry.

Some people will object to listening to voices and with good reason. In later chapters, we'll delve into the ministry of casting out demons. As you've already seen, this has become a very common part of our ministry. Thus it's a regular occurrence for people to tell us they hear voices. The voices they hear bring confusion. They often tell people not to read the Bible, to hurt themselves or others, or to do things sexually that they don't want to do. Some people hear the voices or even see the images of relatives who have passed away. This is not of God; I guarantee it.

Many suggest that any voices believers hear are only our own thoughts—or worse, demons. We should rely solely on Scripture, they say. Scripture is definitely the standard and rule by which every other voice should be judged. But God's voice often fills us in on specifics that His Word doesn't give. God's Word doesn't tell me how to choose between two equally good paths. Scripture cannot reveal specific things about a person to whom I'm ministering.

In my case, early on I was forced to wrestle with whether what God was telling me lined up with Scripture. When God led us to step out in faith and trust Him for our finances, we could argue both for and against it using Scripture. Jesus sent the 12 in Matthew 10, Mark 6, and Luke 9, telling them not to take any extra money, clothes, or shoes. We are not told how long they were gone, but they were to trust God to provide for them.

God's Word also tells us in First Timothy 5:8 that if anyone does not provide for his own, especially for those of his household, he has denied the faith and is worse than an unbeliever. I felt a responsibility to provide for my family and had the ability to make money. But God was telling me that He would take care of our needs and I was to trust Him. If I hadn't learned to listen to His voice, I would never have come to know Christ as I know Him today. I would not have seen God supernaturally enable us to pay every bill in the three years while we lived by faith. Neither of us worked, and we did no fundraising. Every month it took a miracle. You don't live that way unless God has clearly told you to and you're in intimate fellowship with Him.

In Revelation 1, John was on the island of Patmos, and on the Lord's Day he was in the Spirit (see Rev. 1:10). John heard behind him a loud voice like a trumpet. What follows is an entire book that documents what God wanted to speak to the Church about what would take place in the future. The book is filled with visions, angels speaking, Jesus speaking, and glimpses of the future.

In Chapters 2 and 3, we read words that Jesus Himself told John to write for the churches. After each of the seven messages of warning, rebuke, and encouragement, Jesus said, *"He who has an ear, let him hear what the Spirit says to the churches."* The reader is asked to listen to what the Holy Spirit is saying. Jesus is speaking in these passages, but we also have the human example of John, who heard a very specific word for very specific churches. Jesus' strong words of warning must have gotten the attention of those churches; they still command our attention today.

God wants to speak a specific word to His churches today, but if your theology doesn't allow God to speak directly to you or through a word of prophecy to your church, then you'll be like those who do not have ears to hear what the Holy Spirit is saying to the churches. I know legitimate prophets today who are loved by their respective churches till what they have to say is not what the leaders want to hear. Two I know well have been asked to leave their churches by the pastors.

Many theologians and religious leaders quote Revelation 22:18-19 as proof that Jesus has stopped speaking directly to His people today. This passage warns that if anyone adds to the prophecy of "this book," God will add to him the plagues described in it. John also warns that if anyone takes away from the words in this book, he will lose his share in the tree of life. Theologians believe this passage teaches that God revealed everything we need in the Bible. If you claim to have heard from God, they say, you're in violation of this warning and will experience the curse of plagues and a loss of your salvation.

There are many New Age groups that claim to have found a "new gospel" or "missing book" of the Bible. There are some who even claim to "channel" Jesus. The words they speak and write do not agree with Scripture or lead to life. This is what John testified about in Revelation 22.

Much of the Church today has rejected the voice of God and His Holy Spirit because of the fact that some have perverted it. It's like someone who has witnessed a bad marriage declaring he'll never get married. It's like someone who's tasted some bad steak saying he'll never eat steak again. It's like someone who read about a plane crash deciding he'll never fly. But let me tell you, marriage is awesome! Steak tastes great, and flying can save you a lot of time. But none of it compares to hearing God's voice. Knowing that God has said something that someone needs to hear—something you never could have known without His revelation—is one of the greatest experiences you can have.

Marie, a close friend and the owner of a large company, a business-man who walks in the anointing, and I were all in Marie's office on a conference call with two other men. We were talking about business, but I told Danny we needed to pray for Marie because her doctors thought she had cancer and were planning to do a biopsy.

As we prayed, Danny told Marie that he saw her as a little girl, stand-ing on a box and pretending she was preaching and leading worship. Marie began to cry. Danny said that God wanted Marie to know He remembered that, and it was special to Him. He said God wanted her to know how much He loved her heart for people. By this time, Marie was sobbing uncontrollably. Danny then told Marie that God was healing her. The revelation was just a sign for her, to let her know it was God who was speaking. Sure enough, Marie was healed. The doctors gave her a clean bill of health.

Marie will never forget that day and the way God revealed the secrets of her heart to someone else. I'll never forget many of the times when God has revealed things to me that were meant for others, or the times when God healed or delivered them from strongholds.

Learning to hear God's voice involves spending much time in prayer, studying God's Word, and being quiet enough to listen. When believers first try this, many have so much confusion and noise in their spirits because they have chaos-filled lives and other voices clamoring for their attention. Before they go through deliverance, they may hear many voices, and it's always dangerous to listen to any spiritual voice that is not from God. Believers who have listened to demonic voices are the reason why many doubt the validity of God speaking directly to His people today.

Learn to listen. Silence the distractions, and focus your attention on the Lord. It may be good to prepare yourself by reading God's Word or listening to praise music. But turn off the noise, be still, and listen. Most people talk too much in prayer to ever hear God. If there is confusion, ask God to clear it away. If there is anxiety, tell it to go. If there is unforgiveness, then forgive. Whatever comes to mind that may hinder you, ask God to show it to you and deal with it. Don't give up! You can learn to hear the Holy Spirit. Write down what you hear in your spirit. Check out God's Word, and make sure that what you heard lines up with Scripture. Don't ever put what you hear on an equal level with Scripture.

Ways God Speaks in Acts

What are some of the ways God speaks to us today? I recently listed 22 ways that God spoke in the book of Acts alone, so this list isn't exhaustive.

1. The Holy Spirit gave instructions, Acts 1:2.

2. The Resurrected Jesus appeared in the flesh, Acts 1:3-9.

3. Two angels appeared to the people watching the sky, Acts 1:10-11.

4. The disciples cast lots, Acts 1:26.

5. A sound from Heaven appeared like a rushing wind, Acts 2:2.

6. Tongues of fire landed on the heads of the people, Acts 2:3.

7. Believers speak in tongues through the Holy Spirit, Acts 2:4, 6.

8. God spoke through prophets, Acts 3:21-24.

9. Jesus spoke before the resurrection, Acts 3:26.

10. God speaks through preaching through the Holy Spirit, Acts 4:8-12.

11. Believer sees a vision, Acts 7:55-56.

12. The Spirit of God speaks directly, Acts 8:29.

13. A light from Heaven appears, Acts 9:3.

14. There is a direct visitation of postascended Jesus, Acts 9:4-7.

15. God reveals His message in a trance, Acts 10:10.

16. God speaks through a prophet (e.g., Agabus), Acts 11:27-28.

17. Angel smote Herod with a curse, Acts 12:23.

18. Preaching by men of God's Word is one way God speaks, Acts 13:5.

19. Believers speak under the leading of the Holy Spirit, Acts 13:9-11.

20. Scripture is God speaking, Acts 13:32-35.

21. God speaks to confirm His words with signs and wonders, Acts 14:3.

22. God speaks through an earthquake, Acts 16:26.

Ways That God Speaks Throughout Scripture

1. Scripture is the clearest way to know what God is saying.

2. God also speaks directly through *"a gentle whisper"* speaking to our spirit (see 1 Kings 19:12).

3. God speaks through visions, which *Easton's Bible Dictionary* defines as "a vivid apparition, not a dream." A vision is seen with our spiritual eyes. (See, for example, Genesis 46:2, 2 Chronicles 26:5, Job 7:14, Ezekiel 1, Daniel 1:17, Hosea 12:10, and Acts 2:17.)

4. God speaks through dreams. A dream is similar to a vision, but a dream occurs when a person is asleep. (See, for example, Genesis 31:10, Genesis 37:5, Genesis 40-41, Numbers 12:6, Daniel 4, Matthew 1:20, and Acts 2:17.)

5. God speaks through prophets. Prophecy is one of the gifts God gave for the Church. In fact, it is one of the main spiritual gifts mentioned in Scripture (see 1 Cor. 12). Prophets hear from God and speak to the entire Church so that the Church is built up. First Thessalonians 5:20 commands us not to treat prophecies with contempt.

6. God speaks through godly counsel. Scripture often teaches us to seek out godly wisdom from others (see, for example, 1 Tim. 6).

7. God speaks through circumstances. When God needs to get our attention, He sometimes does it through circumstances. But even circumstances are not enough. Just because there's an obstacle in our way, it doesn't mean that God is stopping us. God may want us to persevere through trials or circumstances that seem to be keeping us from moving forward.

8. God communicates through angels. Throughout God's Word, we see angels bringing messages to God's people. (See, for example, Genesis 16, Numbers 22, Zechariah 1, Acts 8, Revelation 5:2.) We are never told that God no longer speaks through angels today.

9. God speaks in person. It was rare that God showed up in physical form to speak to people, even in the Bible. Yet some passages in the Old and New Testaments seem to indicate a physical manifestation of Jesus prior to His birth. (See, for example, Genesis 16, Judges 13).

For each way God speaks, there are counterfeits and perversions. Many people have perverted what the Bible says. Many have said, "God told me to—" and gone on to do things that go against the Word of God. Jeremiah warns of prophets who prophesy false visions and false dreams. We're told there will be many false prophets and that even angels will come and tell us another gospel. Godly people can give us counsel that is not God's will. Scripture is often misinterpreted. Yet are these reasons to write off God's methods of speaking or to say He doesn't speak to us today?

Learn to hear God's voice. Be open to any of the ways God can speak to you today. God longs to speak to you, and He will! Take time to learn and listen. Study God's Word to make sure what you hear agrees with Scripture. We offer thorough teaching on hearing God's voice that can be purchased on our website, or you can become a member and get access to this teaching and more online. Hearing God is foundational for being a biblical disciple.

Study Questions

1. Can you say that you know God has spoken to you? (Describe your personal experience of hearing God.)

_____

_____

_____

2. In the Bible, would you say God spoke often, sometimes, rarely, or never? (Circle one.) Why did you answer as you did?

_____

_____

_____

3. Read John 10:1-16. What does this passage teach us about God speaking and our listening?

_____

_____

4. What does Matthew 10:17-20,27 say about God speaking to us?

_____

_____

_____

5. Why do so many people today reject the voice of God?

_____

_____

_____

6. What are the various ways God speaks?

_____

_____

_____

7. Which of these ways have you experienced God speaking to you?

_____

_____

_____

CHAPTER 11

A Biblical Model for Discipleship

In Matthew 12, Mark 3, and Luke 11, we find one of many encounters between Jesus and the religious leaders of His day. In this instance, Jesus is found healing and casting demons out of a man who is blind and mute. Jesus ministers to this man with miraculous results, but the religious leaders need to find an explanation because people are beginning to follow Jesus. Their explanation is that Jesus has a demon.

The Great Commission

A crucial yet often overlooked and misunderstood facet of the Great Commission is Christ's authority. In Matthew 28:18, Jesus says, *"All authority in heaven and on earth has been given to Me."* This is the foundation for making disciples. Before the commission came the foundation. We must understand the authority Christ has and that this authority is entrusted to all disciples.

Many evangelicals believe that Christ gave authority to His disciples at one time for certain miracles, but that this same power and authority is not available today. This is one of satan's greatest schemes—a lie that causes believers to live in bondage, weakness, and fear.

We are commissioned by Jesus on the basis of this authority:

Therefore go and make disciples of all nations, baptizing them in the name of the Father and of the Son and of the Holy Spirit (Matthew 28:19).

This verse is most often used in churches as the basis for giving money to missions. That purpose misses the main principle being taught here. You won't make true, biblical disciples anywhere if you don't get the foundation right.

The first part of the commission is "baptizing them in the name of the Father and of the Son and of the Holy Spirit." This relates to bringing people to a saving knowledge of Jesus. If we stop there, it's like bringing a child into this world and then leaving him to fend for himself. We must complete the next part, or we are not making disciples as Christ taught us.

Teaching Them All Things

What are the "all things" Jesus taught His disciples? If any of us are to obey this command, we must be able to answer that question.

Throughout Jesus' ministry, three activities went hand in hand. Everywhere He went, the Bible speaks of Jesus preaching the Kingdom of God, casting out evil spirits, and healing the sick.

*Jesus went throughout Galilee, teaching in their synagogues, **preaching the good news of the kingdom, and healing every disease and sickness** among the people....and people brought to Him all who were ill with various diseases, those suffering severe pain, the demon-possessed, those having seizures, and the paralyzed, and **He healed them** (Matthew 4:23-24, emphasis mine).*

*...the people brought to Jesus all who had various kinds of sickness, and laying his hands on each one, **he healed them. Moreover, demons came out of many people...*** (Luke 4:40-41, emphasis mine).

Other references to these three elements working together in Jesus' ministry include Matthew 8:14-17; Matthew 9:35; Mark 1:39; Luke 4:38-44; and Luke 9:11. Yet these are only a few such references. Throughout Jesus' ministry, He performed these three activities in unison.

Any Bible-believing person would agree that this was the ministry Jesus did. They would also accept the next point—that Jesus taught these three elements to His disciples. It's impossible to believe the Bible and miss the fact that Jesus gave authority to His disciples and taught them to preach the Kingdom of God, cast out evil spirits, and heal the sick.

He called His twelve disciples to Him and gave them authority to **drive out evil spirits and to heal every disease and sickness** (Matthew 10:1, emphasis mine).

*As you go, **preach this message: "The kingdom of heaven is near." Heal the sick, raise the dead, cleanse those who have leprosy, drive out demons.** Freely you have received, freely give* (Matthew 10:7-8, emphasis mine).

*They went out and **preached that people should repent.** They **drove out many demons and anointed many sick people with oil and healed them*** (Mark 6:12-13, emphasis mine).

*When Jesus had called the Twelve together, **He gave them power and authority to drive out all demons** and **to cure diseases,** and He sent them out **to preach the kingdom of God and to heal the sick*** (Luke 9:1-2, emphasis mine).

Several distinct things can be seen in these passages. First, Jesus gave His authority to the Twelve. The specific things He sent them out to do are the same things He went about doing on a daily basis. These were not super-spiritual giants of the faith. They were men of normal standing in the community, who had nothing special to distinguish them. Jesus seems to have been driving home His strategy for making disciples.

Jesus' Strategy for Discipleship

We're big on strategy in America today. We look for a church that's growing and try to find out what they did so we can copy it. We write our strategic plans, and the market is ripe because we're driven for success. The question we must ask is "Does our success meet the standard Jesus set for successful discipleship?"

Those who felt most threatened by Jesus and His strategic plan were those who'd been most successful in the religious and social culture of His day. The religious were the most opposed to Jesus' approach to ministry. The same is true today.

The main argument against Jesus having a strategic plan that included preaching the Kingdom of God, casting out evil spirits, and healing the sick is that many believe this type of ministry ceased when the apostles died. They would say that this type of miraculous ministry was reserved for the Twelve. Though I had read the Bible seven times, I too once accepted this belief. Now I've come to realize that this teaching is not true, nor is it biblical.

Discipleship Beyond the Twelve

Luke 10 shows us that Jesus equipped many more than just the original 12 apostles:

After this the Lord appointed seventy-two others and sent them two by two ahead of Him to every town and place where He was about to go.... "Heal the sick who are there and tell them, 'the kingdom of God is near you'" (Luke 10:1,9).

Here we see 72 others who were sent with the same power and authority, and who may have experienced even better results! In verses 17 through 19 we see what actually happened when the 72 returned from their mission trip. We also read Jesus' assessment of what happened:

The seventy-two returned with joy and said, "Lord, even the demons submit to us in Your name." He replied, "I saw satan fall like lightning from heaven. I have given you authority to trample on snakes and scorpions and to overcome all the power of the enemy; nothing will harm you" (Luke 10:17-19).

It's important to note that we know nothing about the 72. We're not told how old they were, their IQ, their social status, or how long they had been following Jesus. Why don't we know these things? I suggest it's because these facts are irrelevant. What Jesus was teaching is that the authority and power were not just for Himself and His 12 closest followers; this strategy was Jesus' plan for reaching the world.

Another Argument From the Skeptics

Some would say we can't accept this as Jesus' strategy for us because Jesus was there to commission the 72. This argument assumes that Jesus is no longer with us and that no one ever did these things except those personally commissioned by Jesus.

The last part of the Great Commission answers the first of these assumptions. Jesus said in Matthew 28:20, *"And surely I am with you always, to the very end of the age."* This statement flies in the face of the argument that Jesus ministered a certain way while He was on the earth, but now He operates differently. He promised repeatedly that He would be with us.

There is also a problem with the argument that to follow Jesus' strategy, one needed to have been commissioned personally by Jesus. In Luke 9:46-50, we read the story of someone who was casting out demons in Jesus' name, who had not been commissioned by Jesus or the disciples.

In this passage, Jesus was dealing with the disciples' spiritual pride. They were in the middle of an argument about who was the greatest. Their hearts had gotten puffed up, and they'd begun to think that maybe they were an elite bunch—and if they were so elite, one of them was surely the most elite. Jesus settled it by putting a little child on His lap and saying that whoever welcomes a little child is the greatest in the Kingdom. He also said, *"He who is least among you all—he is the greatest"* (Luke 9:48). As if that needed an exclamation point, John immediately brought up the fact that there was some guy who was casting out demons in Jesus' name. The disciples had tried to stop him.

Why would the disciples stop a man who was doing the very things Jesus was training them to do? They'd bought into the same lie we've believed if we say that this miracle was only for the Twelve. Jesus cleared up that question right away. *"'Do not stop him,' Jesus said, 'for whoever is not against you is for you'"* (Luke 9:50). This man had realized that what Jesus and the disciples were doing was what Jesus wanted him and others to be doing!

We find another problem with this argument in the ministry of Stephen. The Word tells us in Acts 6:8 that Stephen, *"a man full of God's grace and power, did great wonders and miraculous signs among the people."*

The Bible doesn't tell us exactly what Stephen did, but we know that Stephen was not an apostle, nor was he even an elder in the church. Stephen was chosen to become a deacon and wait on the needs of widows. God's Spirit was operating powerfully through this servant in the church. The example of Philip in Acts 8:6 is even clearer. He was another deacon who is specifically mentioned as being used of God to impact an entire city with healing, casting out of evil spirits, and more.

The Gospel of Mark closes with a poignant passage that confirms the fact that believers are called to do ministry as Jesus did. Jesus says:

> *"And these signs will accompany those who believe: In My name they will drive out demons; they will speak in new tongues; they will pick up snakes with their hands; and when they drink deadly poison, it will not hurt them at all; they will place their hands on sick people, and they will get well"* (Mark 16:17-18).

These verses were included in the canon of Scripture, yet many today argue that they were not part of the original texts but were added later. It is unfortunate that there is such a push today to reconstruct the canon of Scripture. Scholars came against Jesus in His day, and many come against Jesus and His ministry today. Jesus had strict warnings for the scribes and scholars of His day. Yet even without this clear mandate, Jesus' charge is clear. He wanted His disciples then and now to know their power and authority in Christ—and to use that power and authority to do what He did. Jesus' strategy has been and always will be to make disciples who understand their authority, preach the Kingdom of God, cast out evil spirits, and heal the sick.

Food for Thought

Take a minute now to see how your life and ministry stacks up against the ministry of Jesus and His disciples:

1. Preaching the Kingdom of God/Kingdom of Heaven

   • What is the Kingdom of God?

   • Is it different from the Kingdom of Heaven?

   • How can you experience God's Kingdom on earth? (See Matthew 12:28.)

2. Casting Out Evil Spirits

   • How many evil spirits have you cast out?

   • How many messages have you heard on the subject?

   • Is this a normal part of your ministry?

3. Healing Those Who Are Sick

   • When you pray for the sick, do you pray for the doctor or for healing?

   • Are the sick healed when you pray?

   • Is this something people call you for regularly?

I took this test after seven years of theological training and 30 years of church attendance—and failed it. God spoke to me and said, "Richard, you don't know any of the main elements I taught My disciples." That's when I cried out, "Lord, please disciple me!" He heard my cry, and for many years now the Lord has been discipling me. Several years back, the Lord told me, "Now disciple others." Everything I do in my life now must fit into this divine strategy that Jesus laid out. Developing our website was a strategic step to bring this discipleship to more people than we could ever reach with any of our other methods of discipling. A website cannot do every component that is necessary for making true disciples, but it can accomplish a lot. Jesus' strategy was very hands on, and that is what we try to do through interns and in some of our conferences.

Study Questions

1. Read Matthew 28:18-20 (the Great Commission). As you read Chapter 11 of *The Jesus Training Manual,* how does the author define the Great Commission?

_____

_____

_____

2. What were the three main things Jesus did in His ministry? (See Matthew 4:23-24, Luke 4:40, Matthew 8:14-17, Matthew 9:55, Mark 1:39, Luke 9:1-2.)

_____

_____

_____

3. What were the three main elements that Jesus taught His disciples? (See Matthew 10:1, 7-8; Mark 6:12-13; Luke 9:1-2.)

_____

_____

_____

4. Did Jesus pick superstars and theologians to train? If not, who did Jesus disciple?

_____

_____

_____

5. Read Luke 10:1-9, 17-19. What does this passage tell us about the background of these 72?

    a. What were the 72 commissioned to do?

    b. Was Jesus' power and authority reserved for a select few?

    c. Was casting out demons, healing the sick, and preaching Christ's Kingdom what Jesus taught His disciples?

6. Can you find support in Scripture that God has changed His strategy?

_____

_____

_____

7. How did you do on the test at the end of Chapter 11?

_____

_____

_____

8. Ask the Lord to disciple you.

_____

_____

_____

CHAPTER 12

The Believer's Power and Authority

Matthew 28:18 (NASB) reads, *"And Jesus came up and spoke to them, saying, 'All authority has been given to Me in heaven and on earth.'"* How is it significant to us, His modern-day disciples, that Jesus has all authority? How is power different from authority? Do we have authority and power today? And if so, where do they come from? Since Jesus makes mention of His authority in the Great Commission, these are the questions we need to ask as we seek to apply this mandate to our lives.

When I began to explore the authority that believers have through Christ and how to walk in the power of God, I realized that I couldn't remember ever having heard a sermon on these principles. In all my theological training, I'd never had a course on the subject. We never saw any demonstrations of the power of God. Never in my upbringing was this entire facet of ministry introduced to me.

Today I'm amazed that anyone could read the Bible and not grapple seriously with the questions I've posed in the preceding paragraphs. Paul wrote:

But mark this: There will be terrible times in the last days. People will be lovers of themselves, lovers of money, boastful, proud, abusive, disobedient to their parents, ungrateful, unholy, without love, unfor-giving, slanderous, without self-control, brutal, not lovers of the good, treacherous, rash, conceited, lovers of pleasure rather than lovers of God—having a form of godliness but denying its power. Have nothing to do with them (2 Timothy 3:1-5).

When I saw this ominous warning in Second Timothy 3:1-5, I had to admit that my ministry fit many of the traits Paul described. The description that pricked my heart most was *"having a form of godliness but denying its power."* It was an apt depiction of my ministry. I had been to schools and churches that denied the power of God. The final injunction of that passage was chilling: *"Have nothing to do with them."*

I'll never forget the first encounter I had with a person who was manifesting demons. As I shared in an earlier chapter, after I ministered to this student, we sat and talked. She told me that the reason she had chosen to attend her particular church was that she knew the power of God was not there. As I reflected on my own life and ministry, I had to confess that the same could be said of me.

Does Christ intend for disciples to walk in power and authority today?

Yes! In fact, Second Timothy tells us to stay away from those who deny the power. Some might say that "denying the power" means denying that God has power. The same people would argue that this power is not for us to walk in today. Because they believe the miracles happened at one time, they believe they are not "denying the power."

Let me illustrate what denying the power looks like. Recently I was asked to speak at a Bible college. They wanted tapes of my preaching and expressed that they were really excited to have me come. But after they listened to the messages on tape, they told me they couldn't have me as a speaker because I was "charismatic." Though I am involved in a Baptist church and have a degree from an evangelical seminary, because of the fact that I speak of the power of God for healing and deliverance, I'm deemed "charismatic" and thus unacceptable as a speaker at their university.

Denying the power doesn't necessarily mean saying, "I don't believe in the power of God." If you are closed to the power of God, then you're denying the power of God. If the power of God is not active in your church, ministry, or life, then there could be some question as to where you are in the discipleship process.

This is not to say that there is any condemnation for those who are unaware of the power of God and how it can operate through them. When Paul asked the disciples in Ephesus if they had received the Holy Spirit, they replied, *"No, we have not even heard that there is a Holy Spirit"* (Acts 19:2). The problem was not that they were denying or resisting the Spirit; it was a lack of instruction. Most believers would love to know about and operate in God's power, but they are not being taught or discipled in the same way Jesus taught His disciples.

The religious system I grew up in denied the power—or at least redefined it. The power of God was synonymous with salvation. Or perhaps God's power was out there but unattainable for us. The only way we could participate in the power of God was to lead someone to Christ or pray, "If it's Your will." God has so much more in mind for His disciples!

Power and Authority Defined

The Greek words for power and authority are as follows.

Power—*dunamiv (dunamis)*—is found 120 times in the New Testament; dunamis is most often translated "power," but it is also translated "mighty work," "miracles," "strength," and "might." The word can describe both a natural type of power and a supernatural type of power.

Authority—*exousia (exousia)*—This word is used 103 times in the New Testament and is translated "power" 69 times and "authority" 29 times in the King James Version. This word can represent the power of choice and free will, physical and mental power, power of authority or power of rule. *Exousia* reflects the sense of ruling over a realm of authority.

To understand our authority as believers, we need to go back to the beginning of the Bible and God's first injunction to man.

> *Then God said, "Let Us make man in Our image, according to Our likeness; let them have dominion over the fish of the sea, over the birds of the air, and over the cattle, over all the earth and over every creeping thing that creeps on the earth." So God created man in His own image; in the image of God He created him; male and female He created them. Then God blessed them, and God said to them, "Be fruitful and multiply; fill the earth and subdue it; have dominion over the fish of the sea, over the birds of the air, and over every living thing that moves on the earth"* (Genesis 1:26-28 NKJV).

Here we see God's creation as it was intended to be. God gave authority and dominion to mankind to rule over all of creation. Satan had no authority. When satan came into the garden, he was not the ruler of this world. Mankind was given the authority to walk in dominion over all.

In his craftiness, satan came and challenged Adam and Eve to question God. Then he began to offer suggestions of another way. Along with dominion over everything on the earth, Adam and Eve had been given only one prohibition: *"You must not eat from the tree of the knowledge of good and evil..."* (Gen. 2:17). Adam and Eve decided to follow satan's advice and disobey God's command, and thus they gave dominion to the serpent. They submitted to satan and to some degree came under his authority.

Satan had limited power even before Adam and Eve gave him authority in their lives. But satan needed to have authority if he was going to be able to harass mankind. Adam and Eve gave satan that authority by disobeying God. Scripture says that whomever you obey becomes your master: *"Jesus replied, 'I tell you the truth, everyone who sins is a slave to sin'"* (John 8:34). When you become a slave, you give up your authority.

Did God give satan dominion? No! That's the lie of the ages. Since the days of Adam and Eve, men and women have given dominion—authority—to that serpent, satan. All authority is God's authority. God has given us a measure of authority, and we can choose to walk in it or be slaves to whomever we choose.

Dominion was originally entrusted to mankind, and we can reclaim that dominion any time we want. The question is, how do we get it back?

God provided a way for us to regain our authority. God became a man, and as Jesus lived without sin, He never gave satan any authority over His life. Jesus never bowed down, never obeyed satan, and never sinned. He maintained His God-given authority. Thus, He was able to have full access to God's power, though as a man, He had chosen to not take advantage of His deity and lived as a man. By Jesus' shed blood, atonement was made so that we might be clothed in His righteousness and regain our God-ordained authority. We have been given back the authority we once gave away.

From the beginning of Jesus' ministry, we see God who became a man to illustrate what God intended for mankind to do and be. Jesus is our model of discipleship. The standard is high, but the truth is obvious. Jesus walked in authority and power. The crowds testified to His authority as a teacher: *"And they were astonished at His teaching, for He taught them as one having authority, and not as the scribes"* (Mark 1:22 NKJV). The people testified to Jesus' power and authority over unclean spirits: *"Then they were all amazed and spoke among themselves, saying, 'What a word this is! For with authority and power He commands the unclean spirits, and they come out'"* (Luke 4:36 NKJV). And they testified to His *"power to heal sicknesses and to cast out demons"* (Mark 3:15 NKJV).

Under Your Nose but Far Away

A verse I find sad yet intriguing is Luke 5:17:

Now it happened on a certain day, as He was teaching, that there were Pharisees and teachers of the law sitting by, who had come out of every town of Galilee, Judea, and Jerusalem. And the power of the Lord was present to heal them (NKJV).

The power was present for the Pharisees and teachers to be healed, but it didn't fit their theology. The religious community had a hard time with this truth. It's the same today as it was in Jesus' day. Those who've been taught that something is wrong with anyone who claims to exercise authority or power can have it right under their noses, yet miss God's power and presence altogether.

Jesus upset the religious people when He stated His authority and power to forgive sins. Faced with the challenge of a man who was paralyzed from palsy, Jesus dealt this way with the religious leaders:

"Which is easier, to say, 'Your sins are forgiven you,' or to say, 'Rise up and walk'? But that you may know that the Son of Man has power on earth to forgive sins"—He said to the man who was paralyzed, "I say to you, arise, take up your bed, and go to your house" (Luke 5:23-24 NKJV).

The word used here is *exousia*, meaning authority. Jesus is showing us more about the extent of His authority and power. The man had paralysis, but he needed forgiveness. Whether the paralysis was the result of this man's sins or of a generational sin, the text does not say. Jesus may have wanted to deal with the man's real need as well as his felt needs. Whatever the case, Jesus was demonstrating the extent of His authority.

Jesus states something very curious about this facet of authority in John 20:23 (NKJV): *"If you forgive the sins of any, they are forgiven them; If you retain the sins of any, they are retained."* This statement was directed to those who were following Jesus. Was Jesus giving this aspect of authority to His followers? Was He teaching that we have authority to forgive sins?

In Charles Dickens' classic novel *Oliver Twist,* Oliver spends most of his young life living like a pauper and a street beggar. Deep inside, he knows he's not a pauper and that his mother didn't abandon him. It is not until he is much older that Oliver learns he is actually the grandson of the wealthiest man in the city. Oliver's nursemaid not only had lied to Oliver's mother, but she had also robbed Oliver of his identity. Oliver had been taught that he was an orphaned pauper, when in reality he was the son of wealth.

It's a shame that many believers today have been robbed of their identity in Christ. When the religious leaders asked Jesus who had given Him His authority, He wouldn't answer them: *"And He said to them, 'Neither will I tell you by what authority I do these things'"* (Matt. 21:27 NKJV; see also Mark 11:30-33 and Luke 20:8). Most people who will read this have lived the lives of spiritual paupers. But God wants you to know that there's so much more! He not only wants you to know it's available; He wants you to walk in your God-given power and authority.

Do You Have Authority, Too?

In the Gospels we see Jesus giving His 12 disciples power and authority over all demons and to cure diseases:

Then He called His twelve disciples together and gave them power and authority over all demons, and to cure diseases (Luke 9:1 NKJV).

And when He had called His twelve disciples to Him, He gave them power over unclean spirits, to cast them out, and to heal all kinds of sickness and all kinds of disease (Matthew 10:1 NKJV).

And He called the twelve to Himself, and began to send them out two by two, and gave them power over unclean spirits (Mark 6:7 NKJV).

In each of these accounts, we see Jesus choosing 12 ordinary men and entrusting to them the power and authority He had. This aspect of ministry did not cease after one outreach; in Mark 6 we see that Jesus *"began to send them out two by two."* Even after Christ was taken away, the disciples continued to walk in this authority and power.

Lies have kept so many believers from experiencing the power and authority of God. One lie is the teaching that when the last apostle died, so did the authority and power for believers to do miracles. If the passages above were the only ones in which we see Jesus giving His power and authority to believers, then an argument might be made for this. But Jesus said in Luke 10:19:

> *"Behold, I give you the authority to trample on serpents and scorpions, and over all the power of the enemy, and nothing shall by any means hurt you"* (NKJV).

This verse follows the account of Jesus calling and sending out the 72 disciples who will remain nameless and faceless until Jesus returns. I believe Jesus commissioned the 72 in this way to dispel the lie that there would be a limit to those to whom Jesus would give His authority and power.

Jesus also gave this authority to Stephen, a deacon in the Book of Acts: *"And Stephen, full of faith and power, did great wonders and signs among the people"* (Acts 6:8 NKJV). Jesus gave many gifts to the Church. Anyone who would want to limit the power and authority God is giving to His Church today is robbing you of your inheritance.

How Do We Gain This Power?

Scripture says in Luke 4:1 that Jesus went into the desert *"full of the Holy Spirit"* (NASB). Then we learn in Luke 4:14, *"Jesus returned in the power of the Spirit to Galilee, and news of Him went out through all the surrounding region"* (NKJV). Jesus' ministry began after a season of prayer and fasting. We know little about Jesus' life and ministry before this point. There are no recorded miracles apart from Jesus' birth until after His 40-day fast. Several times as Jesus taught, He correlated authority and power to the discipline of fasting. Just because someone fasts, it doesn't automatically produce power in his or her life. The Pharisees were known for fasting, and they had no power. Fasting cannot be a religious activity or out of a desire for a power trip.

Fasting definitely impacts our lives, draws us closer to God, and opens us up to experience more of God's power. Yet as far as we know, the disciples never did a 40-day fast. Matthew 17:21 and Luke 9:40 record an instance in which the disciples were trying and failing to cast demons out of a little boy. Jesus told them that "this type" of demon would only come out as a result of prayer and fasting. In both accounts, Jesus correlated faith—or rather, their lack thereof—as well as their lack of prayer and fasting with the failure to cast out evil spirits. Faith is a prerequisite to ministering in the power of God.

I remember well that during my first extended fast, God strengthened my faith and taught me much from His Word. I had begun to believe that all of God's Word was true and that He wanted me to become His disciple. At the end of that fast, I had my first successful encounter with the demonic. Never before had I operated in God's power in that way, nor had I seen anyone cast out a demon. I had only recently begun to believe that deliverance was part of biblical discipleship and had not read a single book on the subject. What a gracious God we have! To begin to experience this new level of authority, all I had done was take Jesus at His word and ask Him to disciple me. Jesus had been faithful to work in my heart and life, and He entrusted me with His power and authority.

Jesus' method of teaching the disciples about their authority and power was discipleship. He didn't lecture them on the importance of casting out demons or give seven easy steps to setting captives free. Jesus called them to come alongside Him and watch. After a period of watching and listening, Jesus commissioned them to do what they had seen. We at Operation Light Force never let anyone minister at our Healing Conferences or do one-on-one ministry who has not first been ministered to and who has not observed others ministering. The process is simple and the learning curve easy, but the best way to learn is through experience, observation, and practice.

In past years, I have discipled many in the things God taught me over the course of three years about His authority and power. The members of one small group I discipled felt their faith grow immeasurably and learned to walk in victory and power. When we minister at one of our Healing Conferences or one on one, these friends are the backbone of the team that operates in God's authority and power to set others free from strongholds and bondage.

Jesus learned to watch and listen to what God the Father was doing. This is part of what He was teaching us about walking in authority and power. Jesus made it clear that even His authority came from His Father:

"For I have not spoken on My own authority; but the Father who sent Me gave Me a command, what I should say and what I should speak" (John 12:49 NKJV; see also John 14:10).

In order to walk in power and authority, we must have humble, dependent hearts. Whenever we think that the power and authority resides in us, we begin to get off track.

The Great Promise

Behold, I send the Promise of My Father upon you; but tarry in the city of Jerusalem until you are endued with power from on high (Luke 24:49 NKJV).

You've heard of the Great Commandment and the Great Commission; now receive the Great Promise. The "Promise of My Father" was that the Church would be endued with power from on high. Some would say that this power was only given to the disciples, but the same people would teach that the Great Commission is for all believers. Don't accept the lie that the Great Promise isn't for Jesus' disciples today. Jesus has given to His Church power and authority beyond anything you've imagined. He intends for us always to walk in our God-given power and authority.

Others would have you believe that the power Jesus spoke of is only the power to share the Gospel. Luke 24:49 in no way limits the power to sharing the Gospel. If Jesus had intended for ministry and discipleship to be what we do in church when we give an altar call and have people pray a prayer, then that's exactly what He would have done and taught His disciples to do!

Acts 1:8 is a favorite passage of many believers, but don't miss the fact that we are to receive power:

"But you shall receive power when the Holy Spirit has come upon you; and you shall be witnesses to Me in Jerusalem, and in all Judea and Samaria, and to the end of the earth" (NKJV).

Jesus' strategy for impacting the world has never changed. We are to minister today in the same power and authority with which Jesus equipped His disciples.

Paul even prayed this for the Church in Rome, saying:

Now may the God of hope fill you with all joy and peace in believing, that you may abound in hope by the power of the Holy Spirit (Romans 15:13 NKJV).

Paul wanted the Church to experience the power of the Holy Spirit! He testified to that power in his own ministry in Romans 15:18-19:

For I will not dare to speak of any of those things which Christ has not accomplished through me…in mighty signs and wonders, by the power of the Spirit of God, so that from Jerusalem and round about to Illyricum I have fully preached the gospel of Christ (NKJV).

Paul's writings are full of the importance of the power of God in ministry, teaching, and preaching.

And my speech and my preaching were not with persuasive words of human wisdom, but in demonstration of the Spirit and of power, that your faith should not be in the wisdom of men but in the power of God (1 Corinthians 2:4-5 NKJV).

For the kingdom of God is not in word but in power (1 Corinthians 4:20 NKJV).

It is impossible to build a New Testament model of disciple-making apart from the reality of the power and authority of God. It's impossible to achieve your full potential in life or ministry until you walk in the power and authority that God is freely giving you. Like salvation, you receive this power and authority by faith. But you will have to be discipled and taught how to walk in these things. If your spiritual leaders do not walk in their power and authority, how can they teach you? If you cannot find someone, then ask God to disciple you. He may lead you to others who have learned more about walking as children of the King. We as a ministry have sought to put the resources necessary to learn more about your authority and power on our website and through our discipleship resources. Other ministries have valuable resources. Don't give excuses for not walking in *all* of your inheritance.

Don't simply accept what you hear from others. Search the Scriptures for yourself, and judge what others tell you by the Word of God. Next you must begin to appropriate the authority and power in your own life. After you experience the authority and power of God operating through you, it's time to begin entrusting to others what Christ has been teaching you.

Study Questions

1. Read Second Timothy 3:1-5. How does this passage relate to what you see in the religious systems of our day? Your own life?

_____

_____

_____

2. Does Christ intend for disciples to walk in power and authority today?

_____

_____

_____

3. How do Christians and churches deny God's power today?

_____

_____

_____

4. What is the difference in Scripture between the word *power* and the word *authority*?

_____

_____

_____

5. According to Genesis 1:26-28, who did God give dominion to? Who gave dominion to satan, and how?

_____

_____

_____

6. Why do most Christians live lives of spiritual paupers if Jesus has given us authority and power?

_____

_____

_____

7. Has Christ made His authority and power available to us?

_____

_____

_____

8. What are some ways to grow in our experience of God's power for us today?

_____

_____

_____

CHAPTER 13

The Believer's Weapons

For though we walk in the flesh, we do not war according to the flesh. For the weapons of our warfare are not carnal but mighty in God for pulling down strongholds, casting down arguments and every high thing that exalts itself against the knowledge of God, bringing every thought into captivity to the obedience of Christ... (2 Corinthians 10:3-5 NKJV).

It's there in the Bible, but it doesn't suit today's Christianity, does it? We've learned "better ways" to grow a church, with our marketing campaigns and strategies devoid of power. Prayer meetings are often replaced by some form of entertaining "outreach" that appeals to our carnal nature. Not that marketing is of the devil or that fun outreaches don't have value, but if we're relying on this type of strategy to grow the church, then we've missed the most powerful methods outlined in Scripture.

Paul tells us in Second Corinthians 10:3 (NKJV) that even *"though we walk in the flesh, we do not war according to the flesh."* When Paul speaks here of the flesh, he is referring to the soul. The soul is composed of the mind, will, and emotions. Paul tells us that while each of us has a mind, will, and emotions and that these are part of our moment-by-moment reality, they are not sufficient for winning a spiritual battle.

The first reality we must accept is that we are in a spiritual battle. To many of you, this will seem quite obvious. To others, it's a major hurdle. Many can accept what they think, see, and feel but have a hard time admitting to a reality outside their five senses. Nearly all believers speak of the reality of a spiritual realm, but few have much practical understanding of how the spiritual realm intersects with their daily lives. If the spiritual reality is the highest reality, then it is urgent for us to gain a greater understanding of how to relate to the spiritual.

Next we must realize that God has equipped us with both the weapons and the protection needed to wage a spiritual battle. If we are ignorant of these spiritual weapons, we will try to win our daily battles using our natural resources and never tap into the supernatural ones God has given us. Most Christians would say, "I prayed about it, but nothing happened." We give the spiritual weapons a shot, then go back to trying in our strength, understanding, and will to battle our unseen foe. Other Christians try everything first—and then resort to prayer. In most cases, if these believers were honest, they'd have to admit that their prayers made little or no impact. The reason we don't see the sick healed regularly is that our understanding is shallow and our faith weak. The reason most believers live in defeat is that they don't know a thing about their weapons or how to use them.

The NIV translates "the flesh" in Second Corinthians 10:3 as "the world." In other words, our weapons are not the weapons of this world, and we do not wage war as the world does. But the reality is that too often the Church learns its strategies from the world. We are so enamored by the way the world does its thing that we seek to copy the latest late-night TV or music video format, and we think we are accomplishing more. Never in history has the Church been more successful at adopting the world's format, formulas, and glitz—and never has the Church been so lacking in righteousness, power, and life-transforming ministry.

The Weapons of This World

Can you battle the spiritual with the intellect? Can you battle the spiritual with drugs? Can you battle the spiritual with emotive therapy? Today we trust more in science than in the power of God. We pay counselors thousands of dollars to listen to our stories and help us understand what's going on inside, when the real problems have spiritual roots from which only God can free us. Even Christian counselors, if they don't know the power of God, will rely on their training and operate out of the mind, will, and emotions to battle the unseen forces at work in their clients.

People today take medication to handle depression, control their children, stem violence, and deal with pain—yet these medications only numb the pain and deal with the symptoms. They will never touch the spiritual roots of a problem. I have seen people who have never again had to take a pill once the weapons of God were used to deal with the spiritual roots of the matter. Carnal weapons can never heal us of problems that have a spiritual source.

Unless we recognize the spiritual dimension and learn to win the spiritual battles first, we will live in defeat and pay for solutions that don't work.

Divine Power to Demolish Strongholds

In order for believers to minister as God intends for us to, we must get a hold of God's divine power and the weapons He has provided. The apostle Paul teaches us that our weapons have *"divine power to demolish strongholds"* (2 Cor. 10:4). It's difficult to minister to other people's strongholds when strongholds bind our own lives.

What Are Strongholds?

The Theological Dictionary of New Testament Terms defines a stronghold as: (1) a castle, stronghold, fortress, fastness; or, (2) anything on which one relies. A stronghold is anything in our lives—positive or negative—that has become our reliance. If God is who we rely on for strength, then He is our stronghold.

Some harmful strongholds are obvious. Drugs, alcohol, or sex can take over a person's life as he becomes addicted to these powerful influences. These kinds of strongholds often lead a person to the point of destruction. But other less obvious strongholds can have the same destructive effect. Some people rely on caffeine and look to it for strength, not realizing that instead of giving them energy, it robs them of their energy and creates a demand for more caffeine. Some rely on a person. Whether a spouse, a friend, a parent, or a lover, they allow this person to have an inappropriate amount of influence in their lives. For others the stronghold could be ego or self-righteousness. This was the problem the Pharisees had. It's a stronghold that is difficult to see because the focus is on getting things right on the outside, while inside there is bondage to sin.

How Do We Get Strongholds?

Strongholds are built in the mind. They are thought patterns that begin with an idea. That idea may be planted in our minds by our parents, our peers, or any individual or outside spiritual influence, like an evil spirit. Sometimes the thought pattern has been developed over generations and passed down. When the idea—a lie—is planted, the door is opened to other lies and influences. The world, the flesh, and the devil can add a host of other lies to support the original idea. Before you know it, the idea has become a thought pattern, the thought pattern becomes entrenched, and the door is now open for evil spirits to begin controlling your thoughts and behaviors.

Some people open the door to demonic influences in obvious ways, such as holding séances or listening to spirit guides. Sometimes the thought processes originated generations ago in a family member who accepted some of satan's lies. These lies became thought patterns and grew into strongholds that were passed down to subsequent generations. These "generational strongholds" are what the Bible speaks of when it says that the sins of the father are passed on to the following generations (see Exod. 20:5-6). Modern psychology did not invent the understanding that traits are passed from one generation to the next. God established this truth, and only God has the divine power to break curses and restore the generational line. We regularly minister to people who are set free from traits and behaviors that have tormented their family members for generations.

Strongholds can come in a variety of forms. Strongholds that are passed from one generation to the next are called generational curses, inherited curses, or generational sins. If your mother was abused and thus became abusive herself, then it is more likely that you will experience the same demonic stronghold of abuse. If rejection was part of your experience growing up, you may have a tendency to reject your own children. In fact, most people who recognize the rejection they experienced do not recognize the rejection they pass on to others. The good news is that you can be free from inherited curses. Even diseases like arthritis, heart disease, and cancer can be generational. Yet many have found spiritual and physical healing for these illnesses as the curses have been broken.

Power to Demolish Arguments

The Word says that the weapons God gives us have "divine power" to demolish arguments. When this truth is lived out in real life, it is one of the most amazing things I have ever seen. As a pastor, I counseled many people and often watched them grasp the wisdom of God for their situation—yet they often left counseling and did the very things that were destroying them. It seemed so difficult to change people's mindsets! But when I began ministering with greater understanding of my authority and dealing with demonic strongholds, I began seeing people give up long-held, deeply entrenched belief systems within minutes.

My counseling did not bring about this transformation. In fact, many people who come to us for ministry have been to counselors for years. They've paid the most knowledgeable Christian counselors thousands of dollars to help change their thought patterns. Using the powerful weapons God has given us, we've seen these people set free from bondage that counseling couldn't touch, in a matter of minutes or hours.

This is not to negate the value of counseling. The goal of counseling and demolishing strongholds is the same: to change the mindset. A counselor uses time-tested techniques and skills and may even pray for God to help a client change his or her destructive thought patterns. The counselor may ask probing questions to find out what those thought patterns are and then help the client develop new thought patterns. That's good counseling. Bad counseling says, "Whatever you want to do, good or bad, we want to help you figure out how to do it."

Utilizing God-supplied weapons to destroy strongholds differs from counseling in that you begin by learning to hear what God's Spirit is telling you about the person's root problem. Then you address where that root began and the spirits that have been welcomed into the person's life. After that, the person is free. The stronghold is broken, the arguments that supported the stronghold are destroyed, and new thought patterns can begin to develop. I make it sound simple—and the truth is, it is very simple. That's why Jesus was able to take ordinary people and teach them His ways. He was showing them how to set captives free. Our ministry team is not made up of PhDs. We train ordinary people just like Jesus did to do extraordinary miracles.

Our God-given weapons have divine power to demolish everything that sets itself up against the knowledge of God. Believers have so much more authority than they ever could imagine. When we get a hold of who we are, who Jesus is in us, and how to use the weapons God has given us, then watch out world! I am watching our city be revolutionized by people learning to walk in God and all that He has for them. If even a few people could grasp these principles and pass them on to others, then our world would be changed. Jesus knew this. He chose people of no consequence or power and gave them what is also available to us. They turned the world upside down. Come join the army of believers who are learning to use the weapons of divine power to demolish everything that sets itself up against the knowledge of God.

Taking Every Thought Captive

When you utilize spiritual weapons, you can win the mental and emotional battles against satan and sin. Drugs can only numb the senses; they cannot truly change the emotions. Psychotropic medications touted as "the cure" are prescribed today by the millions, but they don't cure a thing. Typically, these drugs are meant to help people get a handle on behaviors and thoughts that are out of control. All medications have negative side effects and cost a lot of money. If that's the best God can do, then we have a problem. The reality is that it's not the best God can do. Most believers have never experienced what God can do because the Church is not walking in the truth and authority God has called us to walk in.

You cannot take your thoughts captive unless you understand the keys of spiritual authority, binding, loosing, and taking away the lies and rights that the enemy has trusted. In a later chapter, we will deal more specifically with how to be released from strongholds, as well as how to set others free.

What Are the Believers' Weapons?

Believers have many weapons at their disposal that, when correctly appropriated, will transform the world. I cannot give you an exhaustive list of weapons that are available to believers, nor are the weapons I've listed in any order of priority. Some may not even seem like weapons to you, so I will take the time to explain each one. They should each be used on a daily basis—if not hourly—in the life of every believer.

Confession, Repentance, and Renunciation

The acts of confession, repentance, and renunciation may seem like unlikely weapons. To most people, confession is akin to surrender—and surrender isn't generally the way we think of fighting a battle or winning a war. But before we can get God to work, we have to let go of the darkness. If we cling to the darkness, God refuses to help us.

The psalmist writes, *"If I regard iniquity in my heart, the Lord will not hear"* (Ps. 66:18 NKJV). Before we can pray with power, our hearts need to be clean before God. Throughout God's Word, we are told that when we see wars, famine, terrors, or calamities coming, the first thing we must do is confess our sins, repent of evil, and renounce it as detestable (see 2 Chron. 7:13-15). The first step toward victory is for men and women to fall on their faces before God in repentance. This was the first thing Jesus taught when He began preaching, and it was the message first entrusted to the disciples.

If you are battling with anything in your life, now is the time to allow God to search your heart. If He convicts you of any impurity, turn from it by confessing, repenting of, and renouncing that sin. Renunciation is a powerful step that is often neglected. To renounce a sin is to proclaim it as evil and determine in your heart that you will never again have anything to do with it.

Jesus' Blood and the Cross

Without the blood of Jesus, confession and repentance would be little more than an admission of defeat. Once we have confessed a sin, Jesus' blood covers it and takes away every right with which the accuser, satan, was able to accuse us and hold our sins against us. Revelation 12:11 says, *"They overcame…*[the devil] *by the blood of the Lamb…."*

I'll never forget the day when I was praying over a pastor to cast out the evil spirits that were tormenting him. The first spirit I addressed said in a mocking voice, "Who does this guy think he is?" Normally that would rattle a person's cage! Had this happened to me three years earlier, I'd have run away and not looked back. I had no authority, no power or faith for that kind of thing. But instead I got a big grin on my face, chuckled back at the enemy, and spoke to that spirit with total confidence: "This guy (me) knows exactly who he is! I am nothing, with no authority in myself and no righteousness to claim in myself. But Jesus Christ is right here with me. You know who He is. He's forgiven me of all my sins, covered me with His righteousness, and filled me with His authority and power. I put you on notice right now that your time is up. You have been found out, and it's time to leave!" The pastor then jerked in his seat a little and shook his head. When I asked him what happened, he said, "The voices in my head said, 'We're out of here!'"

Jesus' blood is more powerful than we can imagine. Paul did an incredible job of laying this out for us in Colossians.

…giving thanks to the Father who has qualified us to be partakers of the inheritance of the saints in the light. He has delivered us from the power of darkness and conveyed us into the kingdom of the

Son of His love, in whom we have redemption through His blood, the forgiveness of sins. He is the image of the invisible God, the firstborn over all creation. For by Him all things were created that are in heaven and that are on earth, visible and invisible, whether thrones or dominions or principalities or powers. All things were created through Him and for Him. And He is before all things, and in Him all things consist. And He is the head of the body, the church, who is the beginning, the firstborn from the dead, that in all things He may have the preeminence. For it pleased the Father that in Him all the fullness should dwell, and by Him to reconcile all things to Himself, by Him, whether things on earth or things in heaven, having made peace through the blood of His cross. And you, who once were alienated and enemies in your mind by wicked works, yet now He has reconciled in the body of His flesh through death, to present you holy...and blameless, and above reproach in His sight (Colossians 1:12-22 NKJV).

Let's look at what God has done for us through Jesus' death and resurrection. He has:

1. Qualified us to receive the inheritance of the saints in the light;

2. Delivered us from the kingdom of darkness into the kingdom of light;

3. Given us redemption and the forgiveness of sins;

4. Made us holy, blameless, and above reproach, or as the NIV states in Colossians 1:22, *"holy...without blemish and free from accusation."*

Wow! We have been qualified, so His blood makes us good enough. We qualify to receive the inheritance of the saints. We don't qualify because we've lived up to some standard or finally have been good on our own. Jesus qualifies us. Our inheritance is spoken of in Scripture as an incredible blessing. Not only is it the inheritance of a place in Heaven; It's an inheritance that entitles us to many other benefits. In fact, if you want a worthwhile study, read the Scriptures that relate to your inheritance in Christ Jesus.

Next, we discover that we've been delivered from one kingdom into another. We have been taken from darkness into light. In today's vernacular, we often speak of "paradigm shifts." That's what walking in God's Kingdom is like. For me, although I grew up in church and went to Bible college and seminary, I learned that God's Kingdom is radically different from my paradigm. If you study God's Kingdom in Scripture and are honest, you will likely experience a paradigm shift as you discover what Christianity is really meant to be.

Finally, we learn that Jesus gave us redemption and forgiveness of sin. In other words, we have been bought back by Jesus, who offered His life for us. His sacrifice is what makes it possible for us to walk in God's Kingdom. His blood has made it feasible for God to be holy and just, yet still forgive us of our sin and debt.

What does Colossians 1:12-22 teach us about who Jesus is?

1. He is the image of the invisible God.

2. He is the firstborn over all creation.

3. He created all things in Heaven and on earth.

4. All things were made for Him.

5. He is before all things, and in Him all things consist.

6. He is the head of the Church.

7. He is the only one to rise from the dead on His own.

8. All God's fullness dwells in Him.

9. He reconciles all things to God.

10. He shed His blood for us.

11. Now He can present us holy, blameless to God.

It is critical that you come to understand who Jesus is. In spiritual warfare, this is 99 percent of the battle. When we understand who Jesus is and what He has done for us, in us, and on our behalf, then we will become powerful tools for God. It's not merely an intellectual understanding of Jesus that we need. We need a practical theology—a theology we can put into practice.

Jesus is God. He existed before creation and was involved in creation at the highest level. Everything was made for Him. He is the highest, the greatest, and the most powerful. He holds the entire world together. Jesus is the head—the CEO—the Chief Shepherd of the Church. Jesus is the only one who has risen from the dead on His own authority and power. You can find the tombs of all other prophets and religious leaders, but not Jesus' tomb. In Jesus is all of the fullness of God. By His blood shed for us, Jesus has reconciled all things to God. Now we come before God as holy and blameless. Why? Because Jesus' blood makes us holy and blameless. We can have authority again because of Jesus' blood. We can overcome the devil because of Jesus' blood. Indeed, there is power in the blood of Jesus!

It is critical to recognize that Jesus is also the head of the Church. In a practical sense, congregations today typically pay someone to be the head of the church. Jesus is no more the head of a given church than the person in charge allows Him to be by walking with Him and obeying Him.

In Colossians 2 we learn even more about what God has done in and for us:

> ...God made you alive with Christ. He forgave us all our sins, having canceled the written code, with its regulations, that was against us and that stood opposed to us; He took it away, nailing it to the cross. And having disarmed the powers and authorities, He made a public spectacle of them, triumphing over them by the cross (Colossians 2:13-15).

Through the Cross:

1. God made you alive with Christ.

2. He forgave all our sins.

3. He canceled the written code that was against us.

4. He nailed our sin and punishment to the Cross.

5. He disarmed the powers and authorities.

6. He made a public spectacle over them.

We need to remind ourselves daily of these truths and begin to understand how to minister the power of Jesus' cross and blood. These are more than theological concepts or words. They are powerful weapons that, when used correctly, can overcome the evil one. Most believers have no idea of the implications of who they are in Christ or what they are equipped to do.

If we truly understand who Jesus is and what He has done, then we cannot help but be overcomers. Jesus' finished work on the cross not only makes us fit for salvation, but it also makes us powerful in battle against satan and his kingdom of darkness. Just as Jesus set captives free, He has given us a ministry of setting captives free.

Testimonies

Revelation 12:11 says, *"They overcame…*[the devil] *by the blood of the Lamb and by the word of their testimony."* Our testimony is not just the story of the time we prayed to receive Jesus. Our testimony is the story of what God has done and is still doing in our lives. If the only thing we can reflect on is a point many years ago when we prayed a simple prayer, then we don't have a present testimony of what God is doing today.

There is nothing more powerful in drawing people to God or over-coming the enemy's work in our lives than a powerful testimony of God's present work. I'll never forget the day when two Jehovah's Witness missionaries came to my door. I had been working in my office, and these two missionaries—one an older, gray-haired gentleman and the other a younger, African-American man—were handing out literature.

I told the men at my door that I'd be glad to take their material but that I wouldn't be able to read it. When they asked why not, I said that I liked to go straight to God's Word as my source. I asked them if they read the Bible, and they told me they did. I asked if they liked the stories about Jesus and the apostles healing the sick and casting out evil spirits. Then I asked what they'd think if I told them that right there in my living room, someone had been healed of cancer and we had cast out evil spirits that week. They said they didn't believe that God does that today. They also said that the devil can fake all the miracles of God. So I asked them if satan was more powerful than their God. They quickly said, "No!" I told them that when they began to experience the Bible they claimed to believe, I would sit down and listen to them.

At this point, the younger man had tears in his eyes, and I detected a hunger for what I was describing. The older gentleman was seething. They had been at my door for nearly 40 minutes, listening to me share testimonies of what God had done. They had no stories of God's past or present activity in their lives.

We need to be in constant relationship with God and telling the stories of what He is doing right now in our lives. Part I of this book is my testimony of what God is doing here and now in my life. I use my testimony and God's Word to share the story of what God is doing to rebuild my faith again and again. I tell the awesome deeds of God to my children so that they can know the same God I know, and believe Him for miracles in their own lives.

Moses challenged the Israelites to remember and retell the things of God to their children. This admonition is for believers today as well. In Deuteronomy 4:9 we are told:

Only be careful, and watch yourselves closely so that you do not forget the things your eyes have seen or let them slip from your heart as long as you live. Teach them to your children and to their children after them.

When the children of Israel became content and forgot their God, He sent them warnings and disaster to get them to turn their hearts back to Him. When they turned back to God, He again did extraordinary miracles on their behalf. God wants to do extraordinary miracles for us all the time. If we remind ourselves often of what Christ has done and can do, we will begin to see God do exciting things in our midst.

God's Word—The Sword of the Spirit

Scripture—particularly a right understanding of God's Word—is one of the most powerful weapons we have. Ephesians 6:17 lists the *"sword of the Spirit"* among the pieces of armor with which believers can defeat the evil one. It is critical that we spend time in God's Word every day and grow in our understanding of it.

It's also critical to develop a biblical theology of any subject you are reading about or studying. Many teachers of the Bible have never even studied the subjects they speak about with confidence. In my freshman Bible class at a denominational college, I heard all kinds of things that undermined my belief in God's Word. It became apparent that the teacher did not believe that the Bible is truly God's Word. Much of the Bible had been explained away as good stories that were much like the myths that were rampant in ancient times.

We were taught that Moses didn't write the first five books of the Bible, that the Red Sea didn't part, that Jonah was not really swallowed by a fish, and other interesting things that were lies. One day after class, I asked the professor if he read the Bible. He looked at me incredulously and asked, "What kind of a question is that?" I repeated the question, and he answered, "I teach the Bible." I asked again, "But do you read the Bible?" Obviously avoiding my question, he claimed he didn't understand what I was getting at. I said, "Has it been years since you read the Bible yourself?" He admitted that it had been years since he'd read the Book he was attempting to teach.

One of my secretaries was in an inductive Bible study at her church, and they were teaching that healings and miracles ended when the last apostle died. I, too, had been taught that in seminary. I told my secretary I could guarantee that her teacher had never read all the passages about healing in God's Word and developed a biblical theology of healing and miracles. He was simply giving her what He had been taught from others. If you can simply write off any part of God's Word, why would you want to study it? It doesn't matter how many degrees you have or how many books you've read on a subject; if you haven't studied God's Word on a subject, don't pretend to teach it to others.

The Name of Jesus

The name of Jesus is not just the tag we put at the end of every prayer. Again, we must search God's Word and see the significance of Jesus' name and its use in prayer. Jesus' name is an incredibly powerful weapon for the believer, yet it is seldom understood.

Throughout the Bible, we find many names of God and His Son, Jesus. God is called Elohim, El Shaddai, Jehovah Rapha, Jehovah Shalom, Jehovah Tsidkenu, Jehovah Shammah, I Am, and many other names.

Each of God's names speaks of a different facet of His character. His names describe what He does and who He is.

The Bible has many names for Jesus as well. Each of His names describes an aspect of who He is or what He does. Jesus is called Emmanuel, the Morning Star, the Door, the Bread of Life, the Son of God, the Light of the World, the Resurrection and the Life, the Vine, the Good Shepherd, the Way, the Truth, and the Life. Each of these names signifies some facet of the truth regarding Jesus.

The New Testament is full of promises and warnings associated with ministering in Jesus' name. In example after example, we see the disciples baptizing in Jesus' name (see Acts 2:38); healing in Jesus' name (see Acts 3:6); teaching and/or preaching in Jesus' name (see Acts 4:18; 5:40; 8:12; 9:27); casting out evil spirits in Jesus' name (see Acts 16:18); and being arrested, beaten, and thrown in jail for ministering in Jesus' name.

In Acts 3, we read the account of a crippled beggar who sat by the gates of the temple. Peter and John were going to the temple at the time of prayer, when this beggar saw them coming and asked for some money. Peter and John looked at the beggar, and Peter told the man to look straight at them. "Silver or gold I do not have, but what I have I give you," said Peter. "In the name of Jesus Christ of Nazareth, walk." Then Peter grabbed the man by the right hand and helped him to his feet. The beggar was healed and began to walk and jump and praise God.

The crowds were amazed at the miracle, but Peter set them straight. He explained that this miracle did not happen because of Peter's and John's own power or godliness (see Acts 3:12). Instead, this miracle occurred to glorify Jesus (see Acts 3:13) and came by faith in Jesus' name (see Acts 3:16).

Do you have to use the phrase "in Jesus' name" every time you pray, or must every miracle be preceded by this or another set of words? The answer is no. The words themselves are not some magical incantation. In Acts 14:9, when Paul saw a crippled man who *"had faith to be healed,"* the Scriptures do not record that Paul used these words. But when God performed the miracle and the crowds wanted to praise Paul and sacrifice to him, Paul told them that the miracle came from God and deflected the glory away from himself.

Speaking the power and authority of Jesus' name and righteousness can be as much for our benefit as for anyone else's when we pray or minister. I've found that when praying for healing or casting out evil spirits, it helps to restate the obvious: "I don't expect this miracle because of my own goodness or righteousness or because of any power in my name. Instead, I believe in the name of Jesus Christ of Nazareth and what He did on the Cross to cover my sins and the sins of the world. I come in His power and am covered in His righteousness." This reminds me of who I am; it also reminds any spirit of who He is and that it has to obey Jesus in me. In Jesus, I become powerful. I have authority and walk in His righteousness. In myself there is no power, no healing or authority—only self-righteous rags.

Learn to speak of Jesus' name and all that it entails. Declare that in the name of Jesus, demons have to flee. In the name of Jesus, the sick are healed. In the name of Jesus, blind eyes receive sight. In the name of Jesus, you have power. In the name of Jesus, you are righteous. In the name of Jesus, your prayers will be answered. The more you begin to grasp these truths, the more you will begin to see God do miracles in and through your life.

Authority and Power

We dealt with power and authority in Chapter 12, but it's important to understand how to utilize all of our spiritual weapons with Christ's authority and power. Authority and power are not necessarily weapons in themselves, but they refer to the manner in which we wield the weapons

God has given us. When we use our weapons without power and authority, the enemy knows it and will not fear the weapons we have.

Other Weapons

Scripture mentions many other weapons we can use to deal with our adversary, the devil, and his spiritual forces of darkness. Prayer is a powerful weapon that is capable of much more than we often realize. Fasting is a weapon that most believers have never put to use. Today's Church needs the power that comes only through fasting. Worship is another weapon that is not addressed in this book. Throughout the Old Testament, God called His people to worship, and He clearly connected their worship with victory over their enemies.

God's vision for you is not that you simply gain the strength to defend yourself. God's vision for you is that you take back territory from satan. God has equipped His people to set captives free, destroy strongholds in the lives of individuals, in our churches, and over our cities.

Wake *up!* Christ is in you, and Christ in you is awesome! You have been given everything you need to defeat the kingdom of darkness in your spheres of influence. You are the light that can drive back the darkness in your home, workplace, or neighborhood.

You don't have to live a defeated life. If you are relying on the carnal weapons of this world, you will live a defeated life. Learn everything you can about the weapons God has given you.

I've heard many people say, "You're one of those people who believes there's a demon behind every bush." This used to make me cringe and back down from any talk of spiritual warfare. Now I realize that the forces of darkness don't have to hide behind bushes. Why would they hide behind bushes anyway? We can't see them. They are right in the face of most believers—tormenting them, belittling them, taunting them, accusing them, scaring them. The reason they aren't hiding is that they don't feel threatened. We welcome them into our homes through our books, videos, magazines, games, and computers.

When the U.S. troops were in Iraq, they had powerful weapons and superior strength. If they let down their guard for even a little time, they became vulnerable. The enemy was everywhere, seeking opportunity to attack the unsuspecting. Don't let down your guard. Use the weapons God has given you with diligence and rout out the enemy in your own life and in the lives of those around you.

Study Questions

1. Read Second Corinthians 10:3-5. Discuss the difference between waging a spiritual battle and waging a carnal battle as it relates to the Church today. Which do you rely upon (carnal weapons or spiritual) and why?

_____

_____

_____

2. What are some of the weapons of this world? Think both of the weapons of a military battle as well as the weapons we use to fight with, influence, or control the world around us.

_____

_____

_____

3. How would you describe the differences between the weapons of this world and our spiritual weapons?

_____

_____

_____

4. What are strongholds? How do we get strongholds? How do we get rid of strongholds?

_____

_____

_____

5. Discuss or write down the various weapons listed in this chapter. Which ones do you need to apply more effectively in your own life? How and when will you do this?

_____

_____

_____

6. What are some other valuable weapons that are not discussed in this chapter that are available for us today?

_____

_____

_____

CHAPTER 14

Triumphant Ministry

I used to look at ministry so differently than how I look at it today. I used to think I had a successful ministry if I had higher numbers than the other groups around me. If you're in ministry, you know exactly what I mean. Whenever pastors or youth pastors get together, the first question asked is, "How's your ministry?" What that usually means is, "How many people are attending?" The typical answer is based on the most people who have ever shown up at one time. If the youth pastor had a band and a free pizza party three months ago and 300 students showed up, he answers that his youth ministry is, "Going great! We hit 300 recently." This hides the fact that only 30 show up most nights. Another leader tells the numbers attending his church and they add the people serving in both services two times because it is better to be sure they got counted than to miss someone. Numbers are the name of the game today if you want to win.

If Jesus had been asked how His ministry was going, I wonder what He'd have answered. Wanting to be the envy of the room, would He have said, "Well, we recently topped 5,000—and that's just counting men! The children's program was overflowing, and you know how many more women there are than men in most places, so you do the math"? Or would Jesus have said, "Well, I spend most of my time working with a group of 12 ordinary guys. I'm training them to do what I do, but they haven't gotten it yet"?

The purpose of most modern ministries is to be a mile wide and an inch deep. As long as you are driven by this purpose, reach as many people as possible and get them into the seats, you're considered successful. But I would contend that this isn't how Christ measures success. In fact, it's quite harmful to the cause of building the Kingdom of God. Millions of people are languishing in the spiritual poverty of churches that have awesome programs meeting all kinds of "felt needs" but that do not make biblical disciples.

I would imagine that the church of Laodicea was like many churches today. The Laodiceans thought they were the envy of all other churches. But Jesus, it appears, had a different perspective. In Revelation 3:14, we see Jesus called *"the Amen, the faithful and true witness, the ruler of God's creation."* If anyone has authority to speak to the Church, it's Jesus. He is the head of the Church, yet most of the time we don't give Him control of what goes on there. We have our own plans, purposes, and agendas.

Jesus said to the church at Laodicea:

I know your deeds, that you are neither cold nor hot. I wish you were either one or the other! So, because you are lukewarm—neither hot nor cold—I am about to spit you out of My mouth (Revelation 3:15-16).

You might think this church just sat around and did nothing, but you'd be wrong. It's not the amount of activity or people or money or even the size of the building that points to success. The Laodiceans said of themselves, *"I am rich; I have acquired wealth and do not need a thing"* (Rev. 3:17). This church assumed they had everything they needed. They had money and they had stuff—and they thought they had it all! Laodicea was one of the most prosperous cities in all of Asia Minor.

Churches that are based in rapidly growing middle-class suburbs can grow faster than they can build buildings, especially if they use the right marketing techniques, have a dynamic worship team, and have a decent program for children. You can grow a church without prayer, without the Spirit of God—without God even being involved! There are churches that thrive numerically and have great building programs that don't even believe in the God of the Bible. Why do I say this? Because it's time to ask God what His measuring stick for success is and wake up to the fact that we may be like Laodicea. We may have a higher estimation of ourselves than Jesus does. Remember, these were the words of Jesus to His Bride. He loved Laodicea enough to tell her what she needed to hear.

Jesus told this church that she was *"wretched, pitiful, poor, blind and naked"* (Rev. 3:17). Jesus wasn't cursing this church; He was telling her the truth of where she was and inviting her to join His purposes. She looked good on the outside but was spiritually blind. She had wealth, but she didn't have God's power. She had riches, but they weren't spiritual riches. She had big buildings, but she wasn't clothed with God's righteousness.

It can be devastating to hear God tell you the truth about who and where you are. Before I could open up and allow God's power to work in my life, I had to come to the place where I realized that all my degrees and years of ministry were what the apostle Paul called "rubbish" (Phil. 3:8). I had a Bible college degree and a master's of divinity, but I lacked the power of God. I had 12 years of ministry experience, but I wasn't walking in authority. I had been on staff at one of the largest, fastest-growing churches in the country, but I wasn't walking in freedom and couldn't set others free. I had to admit that I couldn't do any of the things Jesus had taught 12 ordinary guys to do.

But Jesus doesn't leave you devastated. He told His Bride, Laodicea:

I counsel you to buy from Me gold refined in the fire, so you can become rich; and white clothes to wear, so you can cover your shameful naked-ness; and salve to put on your eyes, so you can see (Revelation 3:18).

Jesus speaks of buying gold refined in the fire because it will cost you something to be refined in the fire and experience spiritual riches.

Jesus also speaks of buying white clothes to wear so that you can cover your shameful nakedness. Today's churches tell people, "You aren't really naked, and there's nothing to be ashamed of." In so-called "progressive" churches, you can keep sinning because God's grace will cover it. People cover and hide their sins, keeping them buried. But when we cover our own sins, it becomes impossible for the blood of Jesus to cover them. We think that if we don't deal with sin, it will just go away. Jesus wants to wash His Bride and clean her from her filth. True righteousness is found in Jesus alone. We have to get to the place where we can honestly confess our sin and admit that it's shameful. We have to address sin head-on, confess it for what it is, and repent of it.

In James 5:16, we learn the power of open confession in bringing healing and effective prayer:

> *Therefore confess your sins to each other and pray for each other so that you may be healed. The prayer of a righteous man is powerful and effective.*

Repentance was a major message of Jesus and the early Church, but it isn't as in vogue today.

Finally, Jesus tells the Laodiceans to buy an anointing salve to put on their eyes so they can see. Without the Holy Spirit's anointing, we cannot "see" spiritual truth. In John 9, there is a powerful account of the religious leaders confronting Jesus. Jesus had encountered a man blind from birth and had forgiven the man's sins and healed him. But the religious leaders began to debate the whole thing. Even when faced with all the proof in the world that the healing was real, they rejected both Jesus' teaching and the miracle. In this instance, the truly blind people were the religious leaders.

The hardest thing to see is our own blindness. It's hard for us to admit that there are truths of God we have not experienced or do not understand. It's easier to come up with a theology that explains away miracles, healing, and casting out evil spirits than to dig into God's Word, admit that you don't see, and ask God to give you sight.

Let's look at one of my favorite passages about successful ministry—the sending of the 72 disciples. Remember, we don't know the names, ages, IQs, social statuses, or anything else about these people. All we know is something of the result of their mission and what Jesus said about them in Luke 10:17-19:

> *The seventy-two returned with joy and said, "Lord, even the demons submit to us in Your name." He replied, "I saw Satan fall like lightning from heaven. I have given you authority to trample on snakes and scorpions and to overcome all the power of the enemy; nothing will harm you."*

In Luke 10:1-16, Jesus outlined the mission He wanted these disciples to accomplish. He began by appointing them. Out of the multitude, Jesus picked those who were truly His disciples. We are not told that they had distinguished themselves in any way, but just that Jesus appointed them. He paired them up and gave them instructions. The first instruction was to pray. Jesus told them to pray specifically that God would send out workers into the harvest field. Then Jesus answered their prayer by sending them. Prayer can be a dangerous thing! If you ask God to send someone, He may send you.

Next Jesus told them, in essence, to trust that God would provide for them. In other words, "Travel light." Jesus then prepared these disciples to set the right atmosphere from the moment they entered a house. They were to speak blessing, saying, "Peace to this house." How often have you heard a more aggressive or negative approach recommended? Yet Jesus instructed His disciples to begin by blessing people.

Jesus then instructed the disciples to heal the sick and tell them, "The Kingdom of God is near you." In this particular passage, we don't have a record of Jesus telling the disciples to cast out evil spirits—a common instruction whenever Jesus commissioned His followers or sent them out on missions. We don't learn until verse 17 that indeed these 72 did cast out evil spirits.

What amazes me is that Jesus gave these instructions to those who followed Him; yet today, very few Christians have a biblical theology of healing, the Kingdom of God, or casting out evil spirits. Even professors at Christian seminaries and colleges have never done an in-depth study of what the Bible teaches about healing or the Kingdom. These three concepts are so often neglected, yet they were key components of what Jesus taught.

Results of the Mission

Let's look at the results of the disciples' mission. Verse 17 tells us they returned from their mission with joy—a word that means *excessive exuberance*. I can testify to how awesome it is to cast evil spirits out of a person and see his life transformed before your eyes. To know without a doubt that you have confronted the spiritual forces of wickedness and triumphed will give you joy and build your faith as little else can. The 72 were exuberant over that very fact. They had faced the demons as Jesus did, and the demons fled.

What Jesus said next is stunning. Can you imagine Jesus assessing your ministry by saying, "I saw satan fall like lightning from heaven"? Talk about results! Commentators have a hard time with this statement because they assume it can't refer to the mission of the 72. Using a little "theological gymnastics," they claim that Jesus was talking about another time and another place. But in the context, Jesus was saying, "You're exactly right; the demons submitted to you! Satan himself was cast down when you went out as the army of God to do what I'd commissioned you to do."

Trampling Snakes and Scorpions

Jesus gave an even more specific explanation of what these disciples were capable of. He told them:

"I have given you authority to trample on snakes and scorpions and to overcome all the power of the enemy; nothing will harm you" (Luke 10:19).

What He was saying is clear. Jesus has given us a generous provision of the vast authority God had given Him. In fact, since Christ lives in us, we have all the authority of Jesus Himself at our disposal. This gives us divine authority over any and all spiritual forces. We can trample serpents and scorpions and overcome all the power of the enemy. Serpents and scorpions refer to the demons, satan's spiritual "ground troops."

Demons are disembodied spirit-beings that seem to have an intense craving to occupy physical bodies. We can see in Scripture that apparently their first choice is a human body, but they are even willing to enter the bodies of animals (see Luke 8:32-33). It is most widely believed that demons are fallen angels. When satan sinned against God (as described in Isa. 14:12-15; Ezek. 28:12-17; and Rev. 12), he took a third of all the angels of Heaven with him. Cast down to earth, they began to establish their own realms of spiritual authority. What is awesome for us to remember is that two-thirds of the angels are with us and on the Lord's side.

The only authority demons have is what we give them. Jesus has all authority, and He has given that authority to those who believe, so that we can overcome the enemy. Unfortunately, few Christians have a practical grasp of who they are in Christ and of the power and authority available to them. *This truth is what the devil fears most.* He knows that if the Church understood this, he would be defeated. No wonder the religious community fights so hard against true kingdom authority and power.

Overcoming All the Power of the Evil One

When a strong man, fully armed, guards his own house, his posses-
sions are safe. But when someone stronger attacks and overpowers

him, he takes away the armor in which the man trusted and divides up the spoils (Luke 11:21-22).

Who is the strong man? "A strong man" in this passage refers to a spiritual stronghold. The religious leaders have just accused Jesus of casting out demons by the power of satan. Explaining why that makes no sense, Jesus introduces an important concept of spiritual warfare. When someone has allowed an evil spirit to come in and control certain areas of life, that spirit sets up house and gets comfortable. It builds walls of defense around itself and begins to steal from the person. The spirits people welcome in often rob them of joy, peace, patience, and all the fruit of the Spirit, while they manifest the opposite characteristics. If a person is manifesting anger, rage, bitterness, lust, or other sinful attitudes or behaviors—and if he cannot walk in the Spirit of God—he typically is battling some type of demonic influence.

Jesus explains that the evil spirit is not threatened until someone stronger comes along, overpowers it, and takes away the armor that spirit was trusting in. So who is stronger than the strong man? Jesus! Who lives inside you? Jesus! What is the armor the strong man trusted in? The armor that spirits trust in is the lies that have been believed and many times passed on from preceding generations. Evil spirits can also trust in lies that are passed on from teachers or friends a person has accepted, who may have opened the door to demonic influence.

We fail to overcome because we don't know who we are, who Christ is, and who we are in Christ. Few Christians I have encountered really understand this simple truth. Confronted with an obvious manifestation of the demonic, most Christians would cower in fear. Many have demonic strongholds themselves and don't even realize they have everything needed to overcome them. I love watching believers get a hold of who they are and the authority they have. Their lives are so radically transformed that it's amazing to see.

Nothing Shall Harm You

Why do most Christians shy away from spiritual warfare, casting out demons, and similar spiritual truths? It's the fear that if they mess with the devil, they'll get crushed. Most Christians have a theology that gives satan more power and might than he actually has. They think that if they enter into true spiritual warfare, they'll be beat up and go running home. Keeping us in fear is satan's number one strategy. But Jesus promised that nothing would harm us.

Matthew 10:28 reads:

Do not be afraid of those who kill the body but cannot kill the soul. Rather, be afraid of the One who can destroy both soul and body in hell.

Some have incorrectly taught that the one who can destroy both the soul and body in hell is satan. But the only entity we should fear is God. When we are in Christ, we do not need to fear satan. Jesus told us that the evil spirits tremble at the name of Jesus. If you don't know the authority you possess, or if you've given demons the legal right to torment you, then you should be afraid.

My neighbor had two dogs. The older dog, Jake, was a little mutt. Then they purchased a black Labrador retriever. When the Lab was a puppy, Jake would push the little Lab all over the yard, teaching him who was boss. As the Labrador grew, he lived in fear of the little mutt. As long as the Labrador feared the mutt, the mutt was in control. One day, the Lab wised up to the situation. I imagine it came to him something like this: "Hey, I'm bigger than he is—and you know, I'm stronger than he is! I'm faster, so why do I run? In fact, I could probably pick that pesky little mutt up and throw him over the fence!" Honestly, when I came home one day and saw the Lab chasing the mutt and having fun doing it, I laughed and rejoiced, because for me it was an analogy of a believer understanding who he or she is and starting to defeat the devil. May you wake up to the reality of who you are. May the Body of Christ wake up to who they are.

We need to get over the fear and understand our authority. Yet many Christians have given the enemy the legal right to torment them. If you harbor unforgiveness, you give the enemy permission to torment you. If you watch movies that include witchcraft, sex, or anything that can entice you to sin, then you are opening a doorway to satan. If you have unconfessed sin, unbelief, or other strongholds, then you're inviting torment into your life. But you can shut the door to satan's kingdom in your life. And that's exactly what you must do before you can fully walk in the authority God is giving you.

Keys to the Kingdom

> *And I will give you the keys of the kingdom of heaven, and whatever you bind on earth will be bound in heaven, and whatever you loose on earth will be loosed in heaven* (Matt. 16:19 NKJV).

Jesus Christ did not die on a cross just so we could go to Heaven. It's much deeper than that. First John 3:8 tells us, *"The reason the Son of God appeared was to destroy the devil's work."*

The word "destroy" is the Greek word *luo,* which speaks of a legal and physical destruction of the devil's work. In a legal sense, *luo* means "to void or dissolve a contract or anything that legally binds." In a physical sense, it means "to melt or untie something that is bound." *Luo* is a very powerful word. The same word is used to describe how Paul's boat was broken (*luo*) to pieces (see Acts 27:41)—and how the elements of the earth will one day melt or dissolve (*luo*) by a great heat (see 2 Pet. 3:10-12).

So we see in First John 3:8 that Jesus' first priority when He appeared was to void satan's contract as ruler of this world. Jesus came to break that contract! When mankind was created, God told Adam and Eve that they were to have dominion over the earth. But when they chose to follow satan instead of God, they handed dominion over the earth to satan. Satan is a legalist. Once we give him a place in our lives, he seeks to hold that ground. He's like the unwanted guest who reminds you, "You said I could drop by anytime and have whatever is in the refrigerator!" But Christ made a way for us to break any contracts we have made with the forces of darkness.

Jesus' sinless life (the life Adam was intended to live), death on a cross, and resurrection gave Him the legal right to have dominion over the earth. He broke the contract the enemy once had. And the second thing Jesus accomplished in destroying the works of the enemy was to untie those who are bound by sin.

That's why Jesus said:

The Spirit of the Lord is upon Me, because He anointed Me to preach the gospel to the poor. He has sent Me to proclaim release to the captives, and recovery of sight to the blind, to set free those who are oppressed, to proclaim the favorable year of the Lord (Luke 4:18-19 NASB).

Jesus not only delivered us legally; He also made certain that the literal consequences of that deliverance were manifested. He brought healing, set captives free, lifted oppression, and liberated those under demonic control.

So does Christ *luo* ("destroy, dissolve, break") the works of the devil, or do we *luo* the works of the devil? The answer is yes! Jesus said:

I will give you the keys of the kingdom of heaven; whatever you bind on earth will be bound in heaven, and whatever you loose [luo] *on earth will be loosed* [luo] *in heaven* (Matthew 16:19).

He gives us the authority to destroy the works of the devil in His name!

The Greek word for binding is *deo*. According to *The Theological Dictionary of New Testament Terms*, this word means "to bind, to fasten with chains, to throw into chains, to put under obligation to the law, to forbid or prohibit."

The Theological Dictionary of New Testament Terms defines loosing three ways: (1) to loose any person (or thing) tied or fastened; (2) to loose one bound (i.e., to unbind, release from bonds, set free); (3) to loosen, undo, dissolve anything bound, tied, or compacted together.

We have been commissioned to bind up the enemy and loose the captives. This is the ministry Jesus intended His followers to fulfill. Jesus has given us the keys to walk in both the freedom and the dominion promised to Adam. It is also God's clear intention that we join Him in the mission of setting captives free. The Believer's Armor:

> *Finally, my brethren, be strong in the Lord and in the power of His might. Put on the whole armor of God, that you may be able to stand against the wiles of the devil. For we do not wrestle against flesh and blood, but against principalities, against powers, against the rulers of the darkness of this age, against spiritual hosts of wickedness in the heavenly places. Therefore take up the whole armor of God, that you may be able to withstand in the evil day, and having done all, to stand. Stand therefore, having girded your waist with truth, having put on the breastplate of righteousness, and having shod your feet with the preparation of the gospel of peace; above all, taking the shield of faith with which you will be able to quench all the fiery darts of the wicked one. And take the helmet of salvation, and the sword of the Spirit, which is the word of God; praying always with all prayer and supplication in the Spirit, being watchful to this end with all perseverance and supplication for all the saints* (Ephesians 6:10-18 NKJV).

Who do we wrestle against? The Word of God tells us that we wrestle against principalities, powers, rulers of this dark age, and spiritual hosts of wickedness in the heavenly places. Who or what are these principalities, powers, rulers, and hosts? Most commentators agree that these are spiritual demonic forces at work in the world. To fight this battle, it's vital that we know who our enemy is and how he fights. What is a principality? How do you wrestle with one and win?

What is this power we're supposed to wrestle with? Do we have the power to overcome it, or do we have a form of godliness that denies the power of God? Have you been equipped to battle with rulers of this dark age or with spiritual hosts of wickedness?

If we're in a battle and have to wrestle these, why don't we have "wrestling classes," as Jesus did, that can teach us how to cast out evil spirits? Wake up, Church! It's time for us to learn the foundational truths Jesus taught His disciples, so that we too can be overcomers.

If we prefer not to wrestle, then we'll end up in a headlock. The enemy doesn't care if you don't want to fight. He may not have to fight very hard to control most Christians, but that's only because they refuse to understand who they are and what they are capable of. The Lord wants us to take up our armor and overcome the devil and his forces.

What Is Our Armor?

The Belt of Truth

Satan's biggest weapons are lies. Because he defeats his enemies through deception, we must be fully armed with God's truth, which can combat lies. The problem is, just as it was in Jesus' day, it's often hard for us to distinguish truth from a lie. The religious people of Jesus' day couldn't receive the Messiah because He didn't fit their ideas about God. Ask God to teach you truth, even if your church doesn't.

The Breastplate of Righteousness

Isaiah 64:6 says:

All of us have become like one who is unclean, and all our righteous acts are like filthy rags; we all shrivel up like a leaf, and like the wind our sins sweep us away.

If we try to stand on our own merit or think that by our good deeds we can earn any favor with God, we are trusting in filthy rags. In Revelation 3:18, Jesus counsels the Laodicean Christians to purchase from Him white clothes to cover their shameful nakedness. This was a church that thought it had arrived—that it was the envy of all other churches. Jesus was urging the Laodiceans to stop trusting in their own righteousness, confess their sins, and repent so that their sins would be covered by Jesus' righteousness.

Shoes of the Gospel of Peace

You may recall that when Jesus commissioned the 72, He told them that when they first entered a house they were to say, "Peace to this house." As we go out to share the Good News, we are bringing the message of peace. God has taken steps to bring peace between God and man. Romans 3:23 reminds us that all of us have gone astray and sinned against God. We were all enemies of God at one time, and our hearts were hardened. But God demonstrated His amazing love by paying the penalty we owed so that we can have peace with God. This is just the beginning of all God wants us to share with people.

The Shield of Faith

Hebrews 11:6 tells us:

And without faith it is impossible to please God, because anyone who comes to Him must believe that He exists and that He rewards those who earnestly seek Him.

Faith is the foundation of our warfare. Abraham's faith was evident by what he did, and God counted his faith as righteousness (see Rom. 4:18-22). Faith is not what we say we believe. It's not even what we believe in our minds, though that is a part of faith. Faith is most evident in what we do. When we believe and live by God's Word, we are evidencing faith. When we choose our own way, we are evidencing unbelief. Without faith, you will be weak and defenseless against satan's schemes and strategies.

The Helmet of Salvation

Salvation is not the finish line but the essential starting place. Our salvation is as much a process as it is a decision. So many decisions made at an altar do not last. Salvation is eternal. Many times God's Word reminds us that if there is no evidence of transformation in our lives, we should make our salvation sure. At the same time, when we are bearing the fruit of salvation and living the transformed life and satan comes against us, we can stand our ground with confidence that we are children of God. After all, it was God who created satan.

The Sword of the Spirit

The sword of the Spirit is God's Word. We must read, meditate on, and memorize God's Word. Jesus used Scripture to combat satan in the wilderness during His season of fasting. The interesting thing about that encounter is that satan also used Scripture to attack Jesus and tempt Him. Scripture can also be used erroneously to the destruction of many. Study the Word of God daily to build up your spiritual defenses.

Prayer

Paul ends his discourse on the armor of a believer with a lesson on prayer. He challenges us to pray: (1) *"on all occasions"*; (2) *"with all kinds of prayers"*; and finally, (3) *"for all the saints"* (Eph. 6:18). To a large degree, prayer has ceased in many churches today, and in most churches it is relegated to a few people who pray in a tiny room. We pray before meals or for a few minutes during a service or Bible study. But Paul makes it clear that we are to pray on all occasions, and the early Church prayed and fasted regularly.

What is Paul saying when he urges the Ephesians to pray *"with all kinds of prayers"*? How many kinds of prayer are there? Most of us only know of one type of prayer. However, in the Bible we see mourning; prophetic prayer; intercession; supplication; praying in the Spirit; praying with understanding; earnest prayer; fervent, effectual prayer; sackcloth and ashes prayer; and exuberant, joyful prayers of praise and adoration. There are many postures for prayer mentioned in the Bible. We see people sitting, standing, kneeling, lying prostrate, and laying on hands. There are prayers of confession, repentance, retribution, worship and praise, thanksgiving, weeping for a city, desperate prayers, and many other types of prayer.

Finally, Paul urges the saints in Ephesus to pray for all the saints. James 5:16 says:

> *Therefore confess your sins to each other and pray for each other so that you may be healed. The prayer of a righteous man is powerful and effective.*

Something incredibly powerful happens when believers confess their sins to one another as they pray in faith for their brothers and sisters in Christ. The grip of sin is loosened when we confess it to someone else. Then, when we pray for one another with faith and power, strongholds are broken and we find greater victory over sin.

I have learned that prayer doesn't mean a group of people sitting in a circle, taking turns uttering eloquent but powerless requests to a God who is far away and only vaguely interested. To be brutally honest, for much of my life that's the only type of prayer meeting I had experienced. But that kind of prayer is typically ineffective, boring, and powerless. Having been in places where revival is happening and seen what a real prayer meeting is all about has made me discontented with the typical American church prayer meeting.

When you hear people calling out in desperation for God and see hundreds gathered, all praying at once, it can seem chaotic at first. Once you get past your preconceived ideas and open your mind and heart, you'll find that wherever revival is being poured out around the world, people have learned some powerful secrets of prayer.

In prayer meetings that make an impact, you might see some people walking and shouting, some weeping on the floor, some sitting and praying in silence, others singing, and some even dancing before the Lord. God loves each expression of prayer, and all of them serve a variety of purposes. If any of these are stifled, then some critical facet of prayer will be hindered. Sadly, most believers' ideas of prayer are based on what they saw growing up. Many have never even seen most of these expressions of prayer, nor do they have a biblical theology of prayer. They have a belief system about prayer, but that doesn't make it biblical.

The Rest of the Story

As I wrote this book, this particular chapter sat unfinished for some time. Now I know why. Today I went to the juvenile detention center in Tampa to meet with a young man who was involved in a murder in which the victim was set on fire. The crime was horrific. About six weeks before, this same young man had sat in my office, and I knew God wanted to set him free. I have learned to use my spiritual weapons and minister in the way I believe Jesus taught the disciples to do. God is 100 percent effective. I had offered this young man the chance to be free from bitterness, rage, anger, depression, and drugs. He told me he didn't need help. I told him that I knew he was miserable but unable to admit that to me. I asked him to call me when he was ready to admit it and wanted help. Two weeks after that meeting, the crime I just described took place.

The young man's parents asked me to visit him in prison. He had told them that now he wanted to meet with me. He was suicidal, depressed, and broken. They sensed an openness in him that they hadn't seen before. As I went to meet with him, I knew God was going to do something supernatural. That may seem like an arrogant statement, but my confidence wasn't based on my own abilities. It was based on God's track record. If a person wants to be free and God has a person to work with who is biblically equipped and using his or her gifts, then that person will be free. I don't hope that someone will be free. I don't pray, "If it's God's will." I do what Jesus told the disciples to do. I cast out the evil spirits in Jesus' name. It didn't take a seminary degree for the disciples, and it doesn't take that today.

Effective ministry was elusive to me before I was discipled by Jesus. The sick were almost never healed. The oppressed were hardly ever set free. I had a knack for counseling and could give good advice, empathize, and seek to reprogram a person's thinking. But set them free? No way!

Today when I met with this young man, he was powerfully set free. I ministered to him for a little over an hour, and when I left he was crying, laughing, and hugging me. The things that had been tormenting him were gone. God filled him with joy, peace, and hope. I will be meeting with him more in the future, and he will gain even more freedom. I and several others will disciple him so that God can use him to minister to others.

Before God transformed my life and discipled me, I would have given a great Bible study, counseled, and prayed for him—and nothing near what happened today would have taken place.

Last week, Victor (whose marriage restoration I described in Chapter 9) and I met with Jeff, the son of a dear friend of mine. Jeff was addicted to marijuana, alcohol, and other drugs. He had recently attempted suicide. Jeff agreed to meet with me on a Friday, and I shared with him testimonies of what God has done in my life and the lives of others. I told him that most of the people we minister to tell us that afterward they feel as if they've been released from prison and they hadn't even known they were in one. Jeff said he knew he was in a prison and wanted to get out. I told him that Jesus wanted to set him free and that I could help. He agreed to meet with us.

So on Monday, Victor, Jeff, and I met for a time of ministry. Victor and I began to bind the evil spirits and cast them out, and Jeff was radically saved and set free from many things. Jeff had asked Jesus to save him but had lived a life of bondage, never knowing the power of God to set him free. His mother couldn't sleep that night as she wept for joy over her son's transformation. She swears he's not the same person.

When I got back to my office, I closed the door, fell on my face, and wept. I told God that it's far too incredible to serve Him. I fully expect God to do the supernatural when I meet with someone. He will set them free if they want it. He will fill them if they're ready. God is awesome, incredible, fun, loving, and so much more. Serving Him with His power is better than anything in this world. I've told friends that it's better than the love of a woman, and that's saying a lot! It's better than food! Allow God to break you out of a theology that doesn't allow Him to be God. Let Him disciple you. Make a commitment to take the next step. Do it today. Don't let this become another book collecting dust that you never do anything about. That is why we created our website and geared it toward training disciples. We want to make it as easy as possible for you to take the next step.

Study Questions

1. When someone says that a church or ministry is "successful," what do we typically equate with success?

_____

_____

_____

2. Read Revelation 3:14-21.

   a. How did the Laodiceans view themselves? (See verse 17.)

   b. How did Jesus view them? (See verse 17b.)

   c. What did Jesus counsel the church of Laodicea to do? (See verse 18.)

3. What does Jesus mean when He said:

   a. Buy from Me gold refined in the fire.

   b. White garments to cover your shameful nakedness.

   c. Eye salve so that you might see.

4. If Luke 10:1-19 is Jesus' standard for triumphant ministry, discuss the marks of that ministry.

   a. I saw satan fall like lightning from heaven.

   b. I have given you authority to:

      i. Trample on snakes and scorpions,

      ii. Overcome all of the power of the enemy.

   c. Nothing shall by any means hurt you.

5. Discuss the believer's armor and its significance for triumphant ministry.

   _____

   _____

   _____

6. So what is triumphant ministry?

   _____

   _____

   _____

CHAPTER 15

Discipleship and Healing

God's Word is not silent on the subject of healing. Beginning with Abraham, who prayed for the healing of Abimelech (see Gen. 20:17), there is much about divine healing in Scripture. Unfortunately, although God's Word is not quiet, today's church has been extremely quiet about healing. It wasn't until I was 33 years old that I began to study every Bible passage on healing. I wanted to know what God's Word said. I knew what my church said: almost nothing. I knew what my seminary had taught me—or rather, hadn't taught me. I knew what my denomination said, but what did God say? I knew dispensational teaching, covenant theology, Calvinist and Armenian theology. But what would happen if I read what the Bible said and set those "boxes" aside?

My study of healing has been fascinating. What has been even more exciting is the result of this study. I could turn this chapter into a testimonial of all of those who have been healed since I began to examine God's Word on the subject. It's been incredible! I still have much to learn in this area, but from my study and experience I was led to write *Lord, Heal Me*, a biblical foundation for healing. In this book, I examine the subject of healing scripturally from Genesis to Revelation. I long to pass along my experience and everything that I have learned so others can begin to experience God's power in this area of the life. I have prayed for people with cancer who have been healed, and others have been instantly relieved of severely debilitating back problems. Others have been healed of hepatitis A, B, and C. We've seen many healed of bipolar, schizophrenia, PTSD, OCD, and many other disorders that the American Medical Association says are incurable.

I have also prayed with people who have not been healed or who later died. One of my best friends is blind, and though I truly believe that one day in this life God will heal him, it hasn't happened yet. I pray that before this book goes to print, Lou will receive his sight. If not, would you join us in praying in faith for this miracle? It will shake up a lot of people in our town because Lou is very well known. In fact, would you pray for God to heal his eyes? One eye is now glass, but that isn't hard for God to take out and replace with the real thing.

I don't have all the answers on healing and will only be able to share my observations. Some of the truths I share in this chapter are blatantly obvious, yet I had never seen them until I made a purposeful search of God's Word. It's amazing that we can go to church for years and never hear about a truth so foundational to Jesus' ministry.

I will tell you straight off that the Bible links healing with casting out demons. When I show you that in Scripture, you'll think I snuck in your house and put it in your Bible while you were sleeping! Some of what I'll reveal to you from the Word is blatantly obvious, yet you may never have seen it before. In fact, if I were a betting man, I would bet that more than 98 percent of the people reading this book have never noticed the link between healing and casting out demons. They've never ever heard it in a sermon, read it in a book, or studied it in Sunday school.

Old Testament Healing

In Genesis, we see God heal Abimelech through Abraham's prayer (see Gen. 20:17). In Exodus, Jehovah declares, *"I am the LORD that healeth thee,"* introducing one of His Hebrew names, Jehovah Rapha (Exod. 15:26 KJV). In Numbers 12:13, Moses prays for Miriam, whom God struck with leprosy, and she is supernaturally healed. In Deuteronomy, God declares that He is the only God who can heal:

See now that I, even I, am He, and there is no god with Me: I kill, and I make alive; I wound, and I heal: neither is there any that can deliver out of My hand (Deut. 32:39 KJV).

In First Samuel 6, the Philistines send the ark of God back to Israel so they can be healed of the plague of tumors God sent among them. In Second Kings 2, God uses Elisha to heal waters that were causing death and making the land unproductive. In Second Kings 20, God healed Hezekiah, partly through the ministry of Isaiah. In Second Chronicles 7, God promises to heal the land whenever His people humble themselves, pray, seek His face, and turn from their wicked ways. In Second Chronicles 30, God heals the people of Israel when they celebrate the feasts and Hezekiah calls out to Him on their behalf.

Throughout the Psalms, the various psalmists present a God who heals. In Psalm 103, we see that God heals all our diseases. In Psalm 147, we find that God not only heals the body, but also the broken heart. Throughout Proverbs we learn practical steps to walking in health, such as heeding wisdom, speaking wisdom, and speaking pleasant words.

In Isaiah 6, we see God making the hearts of His people dull, their ears heavy, and their eyes shut so they can't see, hear, or understand and turn to Him and be healed. John quoted Isaiah when he spoke of the religious people who saw the miracles of Jesus, watched Him heal the sick and cast out evil spirits, yet still did not believe (see John 12:40). In Isaiah 53:5, we learn that healing came to us by the stripes Jesus took upon His back when He was crucified for our sins. In Isaiah 58, we learn that true fasting—fasting that cares for the needs of the poor, the needy, and orphans—will cause our healing to spring forth quickly.

In Jeremiah 6 and 8, we learn that God was angry with His leaders when they only healed the people superficially by speaking peace to them when there was no peace. The healing they experienced was nothing more than a false sense of hope. But God's healing is neither false nor superficial. His healing is complete.

In Ezekiel 34, Ezekiel prophesied against the shepherds (spiritual leaders or pastors) of the nation of Israel. His prophecy denounces these leaders because they cared for themselves, ate the best foods, and clothed themselves in the finest clothing, but had not *"strengthened the weak or healed the sick or bound up the injured"* (Ezek. 34:4). The words in this chapter are a scathing rebuke of spiritual leaders who fail to bring God's healing to people, but who instead rule them harshly for their own benefit.

In Ezekiel 47, we see the river of God that flows from the temple. This river is believed by many to represent the anointing of God or the Holy Spirit, as Jesus spoke of in John 7:38-39. In this passage, Jesus described the streams of life that would flow from within those who believed in Him. John clarifies that Jesus was speaking of the Holy Spirit, whom Jesus would send and the disciples would soon receive. Ezekiel tells us that this river will bring healing to the waters they touch. A possible interpretation of this passage is that those who receive the Holy Spirit will have their spirits healed, so that the "water" that flows from within them is fresh. Just as our bodies need healing, our spirits need healing as well. We also see Ezekiel being challenged by the angel who showed him the river and urged him to go deeper in it. We too must move deeper into the realms of the Spirit until we are filled and immersed.

In the New Testament, the injunction is to be "baptized with the Holy Spirit." That's a phrase that sends chills up the spine of many an evangelical. Anyone who would utter the words "baptized in the Holy Spirit" is automatically lumped in the charismatic camp. It's unfortunate that believers would reject a deeper walk in the Holy Spirit—the river of

God that Ezekiel described as so overwhelming, yet bringing so much life and fruit.

Ezekiel's final word about this river is that the fruit trees growing along its banks would produce both fruit for food and leaves for healing. The type of healing is not specified. I believe the reason God did not specify this is that His healing is comprehensive, touching the spirit, soul, and body.

Hosea says much about healing the nation of Israel (see Hos. 5:13; 6:1; 7:1; and 11:3). This prophet speaks of a healing that was available but that Israel would not accept for herself. This is so tragic. In Luke 5:17, the power of God was present to heal even the Pharisees and scribes, but they were more interested in their petty theological differences with Jesus. We hear of the same tragic reality in Nahum 3:19.

In Zechariah 11:16, we read a similar rebuke to that found in Ezekiel—an admonition toward the shepherd/pastors of Israel. Rather than ministering healing to the flock, these foolish shepherds took care of their own needs.

Finally, in Malachi, we find the clear message that if you fear God and His name, then *"the Sun of Righteousness shall arise with healing in His wings"* (Mal. 4:2 NKJV). Who or what is the Sun of Righteousness? Could this also be a reference to the Holy Spirit, or is it a reference to God's Son, Jesus, who would come with a ministry of healing?

What amazes me is that I could spend more than 30 years in church and never hear a message about healing, or that we could have discipleship classes and refuse to explore the subject. I had no idea that the Old Testament said so much on a subject Jesus had taken great pains to teach His disciples. Granted, there may be subjects that warrant greater emphasis, but it's obvious that God did not want us to be silent on the matter of healing. The Old Testament isn't silent. Now let's see what the New Testament has to say.

New Testament Teaching on Healing

The Gospels are saturated with Jesus' ministry of healing. Jesus announced in His first sermon that His ministry would involve healing the brokenhearted. From the very first day of His ministry, Jesus went about healing people of all kinds of sicknesses (see Matt. 4:23; Mark 1:34; Luke 4:40).

If you read the Gospels, you get a sense that healing wasn't something that happened every so often. It seems it was an everyday thing. There are so many stories of people being healed during Jesus' earthly ministry that we find at least one account of healing in more than half the chapters of the Gospels. If Jesus wasn't teaching or casting out evil spirits, He was healing sicknesses of one kind or another. On many occasions there were so many healings in one place that the writer simply summarized with a statement like *"He healed them," "He healed them all,"* or *"healing every sickness and disease among the people"* (Matt. 4:23-24; 9:35; 12:15; 14:14; 15:30; 19:2; 21:14). References like these are found throughout the Gospels. Jesus did so much healing that the stories would have, as John said, filled the world to overflowing had they been written down (see John 21:25).

In close to half of Jesus' healing encounters, He also dealt with demonic spirits. I had read the entire Bible at least seven times and the Gospels many more, but I had never seen that fact. Let me show you that this is true. Luke, who is believed to have been a Gentile doctor, brings this fact out in some of his accounts. Such an incident is found in the passage where Jesus ministered to Peter's mother-in-law. Luke 4:39 says that Jesus *"rebuked the fever, and it left her."* In other words, Jesus spoke to the fever and told it to go. The fever obeyed.

We find another example in Luke 13:10-17—the story of a woman who had been crippled and stooped over for 18 years. In verse 11, we are told that a spirit of infirmity had crippled this woman. In each encounter,

Jesus discerned whether the person needed healing, freedom from evil spirits, or forgiveness.

In Matthew 9:32, we see an example of Jesus casting out a demon to heal a person who could not talk. Jesus cast out the demon, and thus the man was healed. It is very clear that the healing came when the demon was driven out; the demon was causing this man to be mute. In Matthew 12:22-23, we see Jesus healing a demon-possessed man who was both blind and mute. This sparked a debate among the Pharisees about whether or not Jesus cast out evil spirits by the power of satan. It's amazing how many believers can read Scripture and yet believe that it's evil to teach that God still sets captives free today. There is much opposition to these foundational aspects of Jesus' ministry. Yet Jesus told His disciples and apostles to expect opposition.

In Matthew 17:14-21, Mark 9:14-29, and Luke 9:37-43, we see Jesus ministering to a boy with epilepsy; each account gives different details that help paint the full picture. We are told, *"Jesus rebuked the demon, and it came out of the boy, and he was healed from that moment"* (Matt. 17:18). We also learn that a lack of faith on the part of the disciples kept them from healing this boy. In Mark 9:29 (KJV) we discover, *"This kind can come forth by nothing, but by prayer and fasting."*

The ministry of healing was not exclusive to Jesus. The 12 men Jesus chose to pour His life into were all commissioned with the ministry of healing. In Matthew 10, Mark 3, and Luke 9, we see Jesus commissioning them with the same ministry He had. They were to cast out evil spirits, heal the sick, and preach the Kingdom of God. Once they began this ministry, the disciples never ceased to carry it out. Even in Acts we find summary statements like "all of them were healed" (see Acts 5:16; 8:7; and 28:8-9).

Luke 10 proves that this ministry was not reserved for a few chosen men. Jesus appointed 72 others to go out in pairs and minister healing, cast out evil spirits, and preach the Kingdom of God. The 72 had incredible success, and Jesus told them He had given them authority over all the power of the enemy and that nothing would harm them (see Luke 10:19).

Modern theologians try to explain why Jesus' ministry of healing is not applicable today. We are taught that healing only happened when Jesus was physically present. We're told that the disciples could only heal because they'd personally been with Jesus. We are expected to understand that the Bible's historical narrative was not intended to teach theology.

Well, if we believe the Great Commission, which few, if any, deny, then when Jesus told His followers to make disciples of all nations and to "teach them everything I have taught you," how can we not conclude that this means teaching them about healing, casting out evil spirits, and the Kingdom of God? Why would today's disciples be exempt from needing to know what Jesus taught? What did Jesus teach His disciples if not these three elements? Are we making biblical disciples if we neglect to teach these things? Moreover, are we truly disciples of Jesus if we fail to learn these critical aspects of His ministry?

Paul's was a healing ministry (see Acts 14; 19; and 28). He taught in First Corinthians 12 that there is a supernatural gift of healing. The author of Hebrews also spoke of healing (see Heb. 12:13). Peter, whose ministry of healing continued after Jesus' ascension, taught in First Peter 2:24 on the healing Jesus brought us.

We can neglect the ministry of healing as did the shepherds of Israel in the days of Ezekiel and Zechariah. We can sit back like the Pharisees and scribes and debate the concept theologically while missing the opportunity to be healed. We may be considered good evangelicals if we ignore the subject altogether and talk against anyone who even hints at the possible ministry or spiritual gift of healing. But the Bible is full of healing.

Study Questions

1. Would you say that you have been taught a lot, some, little, or nothing about healing? Why or why not?

_____

_____

_____

2. What stands out to you about the teaching on healing found in the Old Testament? Did you know there was healing in the Old Testament?

_____

_____

_____

3. Read Luke 13:10-17. What connection do you find between the woman's healing and evil spirits?

_____

_____

_____

4. Would you believe that in close to half of the healing encounters there were evil spirits involved in the infirmity?

_____

_____

_____

5. Who in the New Testament can you remember were involved in ministering healing?

_____

_____

_____

CHAPTER 16

The Kingdom of God: God's Will for Your Life

*…Jesus came into Galilee, preaching the gospel of the **kingdom** of God* (Mark 1:14 KJV, emphasis mine).

*And as ye go, preach, saying, The **kingdom** of heaven is at hand* (Matthew 10:7 KJV, emphasis mine).

Jesus went about preaching the Kingdom. From the time He awoke in the morning till the time He went to bed, every day that we have recorded in the Gospels, it seems that Jesus was preaching the Kingdom of God, teaching about the Kingdom of God, and demonstrating what it is like to live within the Kingdom of God. Preaching about God's Kingdom is what Jesus told His disciples to do (see Matt. 10, Mark 6, Luke 9–10).

Throughout Jesus' life, He was teaching parables about the Kingdom. On the way to His death, He was even trying to teach Pilate about His Kingdom:

Jesus said, "My kingdom is not of this world. If it were, My servants would fight to prevent My arrest by the Jews. But now My kingdom is from another place." "You are a king, then!" said Pilate. Jesus answered, "You are right in saying I am a king. In fact, for this reason

*I was born, and for this I came into the world, to testify to the truth.
Everyone on the side of truth listens to Me"* (John 18:36-37).

Even after He arose from the dead, Jesus talked to His disciples about
the Kingdom of God as shown in Acts 1:3: *"He appeared to them over a
period of forty days and spoke about the kingdom of God."*

One of the most life-transforming studies that I have done was when
I searched the Scriptures for every passage on the Kingdom of God. What
I found both thrilled me and disturbed me. Even with my first cursory
study of the passages on God's Kingdom, I realized that what Jesus came
to preach, teach, and establish was radically different from what I had
heard Sunday after Sunday and that my own teaching and preaching fell
far short of God's Kingdom agenda.

I have often asked groups and individuals what they believe the
"Kingdom of God" refers to. Invariably, most will say "Heaven." We've
heard Heaven talked about as the "Kingdom of God." Many think that
the Kingdom of God is the place where we will go when we die. Matthew's Gospel even called it the "Kingdom of Heaven." With that line
of thinking, the Kingdom of God and of Heaven becomes somewhat
irrelevant to this life. But most people have never actually studied the
Kingdom of God passages within the Bible. What you will find, if you
take the time to study this for yourself, is that the Kingdom of God is very
relevant. In fact, it was considered by Christ to be His main theme—and
if there's ever been a relevant preacher, it was Jesus. You will also learn, as
you study the Kingdom of God and the Kingdom of Heaven, that most
of the passages are better understood in the context of a now Kingdom,
not a future Kingdom.

I will attempt, in this chapter, to give you a sampling overview of
what God revealed to me in this study. I believe that one of my next books
will be about the Kingdom of God because I cannot do justice to this
topic in one chapter. I challenge you to begin a quest to know, experience,
walk in, and understand the Kingdom of God.

As you study the Kingdom of God, you find out that there are laws that apply to this Kingdom. You learn that this Kingdom supercedes and permeates all other kingdoms. You will find that there is an opposing kingdom. You will begin to be able to evaluate everything by which kingdom is being represented.

The Hebrew word for "kingdom" is *mamlakah (mam-law-kaw')* and it is translated in the KJV as "kingdom" 110 times, "royal" 4 times, "reign" 2 times, "king's" 1 time, for a total of 117 times. Below is the definition:

- 1. Kingdom, dominion, reign, sovereignty

- a. Kingdom, realm

- b. Sovereignty, dominion

- c. Reign

The New Testament word for "kingdom" is *basileia (bas-il-i'-ah)*. In the KJV it is translated: "kingdom [of God]" 71 times, "kingdom [of heaven]" 32 times, "kingdom" (general or evil) 20 times, "[Thy or Thine] kingdom" 6 times, "His kingdom" 6 times, "the kingdom" 5 times, "[My] kingdom" 4 times, and miscellaneous 18 times.

Definitions:

- 1. Royal power, kingship, dominion, rule, not to be confused with an actual kingdom but rather the right or authority to rule over a kingdom

- a. of the royal power of Jesus as the triumphant Messiah

- b. of the royal power and dignity conferred on Christians in the Messiah's kingdom

- c. a kingdom, the territory subject to the rule of a king

- 2. Used in the N.T. to refer to the reign of the Messiah

In the *Young's Literal Translation*, the word *Kingdom* is nearly always translated "Reign." It really unlocks the key to understanding the concept of the Kingdom of God when you substitute the word *Reign* for *Kingdom*. We don't typically use the word Kingdom; therefore the concept can become somewhat lost and the meaning can be missed so easily. Jesus came to rule and reign in the hearts and lives of people today. He did set up His Kingdom here and now, but it was not a governmental Kingdom. It was a spiritual Kingdom. Let me seek to explain some of the exciting truths behind the Kingdom of God.

God Created Man to Rule

*God blessed them and said to them, "Be fruitful and increase in number; fill the earth and subdue it. **Rule over** the fish of the sea and the birds of the air and over every living creature that moves on the ground"* (Genesis 1:28 emphasis mine).

As with teaching of the Word of God, we must go to the beginning of the book to find our understanding. You cannot start at the end. When mankind was created, he was given dominion and authority to rule over all of creation. You and I were created to rule the kingdom of this world. God loves to share His authority, His rule, and His reign with His children. From the very beginning, God intended for us to be like Him in that we were created: to rule, to reign, and to have dominion over all that God created. Ruling and having dominion over a kingdom is part of the very nature of God. We were created in His image, and God's destiny for us was to join Him in this role of dominion. But something went seriously wrong.

Again, the devil took Him to a very high mountain and showed Him all the kingdoms of the world and their splendor. "All this I will give You," he said, "if You will bow down and worship me" (Matthew 4:8-9).

Here we find satan offering Jesus all the kingdoms of this world. *Wait a second!* Why did satan have any right to make this offer to Jesus? When did satan become the ruler over God's creation? In Ephesians 2:2, we see satan called the ruler of the kingdom of the air:

*In which you used to live when you followed the ways of this world and of the **ruler of the kingdom of the air,** the spirit who is now at work in those who are disobedient* (emphasis added).

Ephesians 6:12 calls satan and his demons:

…the rulers, against the authorities, against the powers of this dark world and against the spiritual forces of evil in the heavenly realms.

Second Corinthians 4:4 calls satan "*the god of this age.*" Where did satan get his authority to rule in this world? Did God give satan an equal measure of authority? Why would God give satan rule over this world if He had given it to mankind?

God didn't give the authority to satan. Humans give up their authority when we choose willingly to submit to satan and his will for our lives. Thus the epic battle for this planet, for the souls of mankind and the battle between light versus darkness, began. In John 8:34-35, Jesus replied:

*"I tell you the truth, everyone who sins is a **slave to sin.** Now a **slave** has no permanent place in the family, but a son belongs to it forever"* *(emphasis added).*

Since Adam and Eve, all of mankind has chosen to become slaves to sin and to darkness. We gave over our dominion and our God-given right to rule, not only over the planet but also our very own lives. The very word *redemption* signifies a buying back. We have sold ourselves into slavery by becoming obedient to another kingdom. Jesus came to buy us back from slavery and to reestablish our place with Him.

In Genesis 3:1-7, we find the tragic story of the tempter, satan, who had power, that God had given him, but who had no authority over mankind. Satan made an offer to Eve that contradicted the Word and promise of God and His Kingdom. Eve was in a position at that time to trample that serpent and maintain her position of dominion. Instead, Eve decided to find out what it was like outside of God's Kingdom. She thought that maybe there was something in the promise of this serpent that would allow her to experience more than the perfection that she had come to know. Eve decided to relinquish her place of dominion and become subject to satan's kingdom. Think about it. Eve was called to rule over all of creation and every creature that moves on the ground. She could have trampled that serpent and lived forever in Eden.

I've seen people give over their place of dominion in many places. You've seen it. When a parent allows his four-year-old to rule the home, the parent has given his rightful place as head of the household to a four-year-old. I've seen employers who were afraid to lead their company begin to allow another person in the company to tell everyone what to do. That is what it is like when we are not in our rightful place in this world. We were meant to rule over satan and all of creation, but satan gets his authority and dominion when we fail to take our place in God's Kingdom and rule with Christ.

From the beginning of time, there have been two kingdoms operating within this world. There is the Kingdom of God, where God invites man to operate within the framework of His Kingdom and obey the laws of that Kingdom. Within this Kingdom, mankind is given liberty and is even allowed to share in God's authority as a ruler over all of creation. There is at the same time another kingdom that operates by a different set of rules. The kingdom of darkness promises freedom but offers slavery. It claims to liberate men and women from the rules of God's Kingdom but has its own set of rules that are destructive.

The Exciting News

Jesus came for a very specific purpose, which is found clearly spelled out in First John 3:4-10:

*Everyone who sins breaks the law; in fact, sin is lawlessness. But you know that He appeared so that He might take away our sins. And in Him is no sin. No one who lives in Him keeps on sinning. No one who continues to sin has either seen Him or known Him. Dear children, do not let anyone lead you astray. He who does what is right is righteous, just as He is righteous. He who does what is sinful is of the devil, because the devil has been sinning from the beginning. **The reason the Son of God appeared was to destroy the devil's work.** No one who is born of God will continue to sin, because God's seed remains in him; he cannot go on sinning, because he has been born of God. This is how we know who the children of God are and who the children of the devil are: Anyone who does not do what is right is not a child of God; nor is anyone who does not love his brother* (emphasis added).

Satan in his pride decided that he wanted to be like God and have his own kingdom. Satan began to set up his own rules for his kingdom. He had established his own governmental system within his ranks. In order to have a kingdom, one must have subjects. Since mankind was the main component of God's Kingdom on earth, satan knew that he must begin the process of securing those who would be willing to subject themselves to his plan, purpose, and kingdom agenda.

Jesus came to destroy the devil's work. He came to redeem mankind and to save us. He came to restore our purpose and destiny in this world. He came to deliver us from the kingdom of darkness into the Kingdom of the Son He loves. Colossians 1:12-14 says:

Giving thanks to the Father, who has qualified you to share in the inheritance of the saints in the kingdom of light. For He has rescued us from the dominion of darkness and brought us into the kingdom of the Son He loves, in whom we have redemption, the forgiveness of sins.

Mankind had turned over authority and his God-given right to rule, like a person hands over keys to his or her house. The only problem is that we handed them over to the devil, and he set out to destroy our house. Satan seeks to steal, to kill, and to destroy. Jesus came to offer us life more abundantly. He came to destroy the devil's work. He came to rescue us from the dominion of darkness where we had become willing subjects and bring us back into the Kingdom of light and of His Son, Jesus.

Because Jesus lived a sinless life, He never gave up His dominion that God had given Him. Jesus never submitted to the devil. Throughout His life, Jesus was the only person to maintain His God-given right to rule that was entrusted to all mankind. Even when Pilate was questioning Jesus as He faced death by crucifixion, Jesus maintained that Pilate had no authority except what was given to him (see John 19:11), and Jesus stated very clearly in John 10:18 that He was laying down His life. No one had authority over Jesus.

> *No one takes it from Me, but I **lay it down** of My own accord. I have authority to **lay it down** and authority to take it up again. This command I received from My Father* (John 10:18 emphasis mine).

At Jesus' death, His blood paid the penalty for our sins. Jesus bought us back from our slavery. Through forgiveness, Jesus has cleansed us from all unrighteousness and canceled the contract we had with the devil. We have been restored to our rightful place of dominion over all of creation:

> *Once you were alienated from God and were enemies in your minds because of your evil behavior. But now He has reconciled you by Christ's physical body through death to present you holy in His sight, without blemish and free from accusation* (Colossians 1:21-22).

Here we learn that we have been cleansed and the enemy's right to control us has been taken away. In Colossians 2:9-10, we learn what our rightful place is:

> *For in Christ all the fullness of the Deity lives in bodily form, and you have been given fullness in Christ, who is the head over every power and authority.*

The fullness of the deity dwells in Christ, and Christ dwells in us, and we have been given His fullness. Jesus is the head over every power and authority.

Wow! Stop and ponder this! *Wow!*

You! Yes, you! If you are in Christ, you have been entrusted with the fullness of the deity of Christ, and as such, you join Him in a position that is above every power and authority. Stop running and hiding from the devil and his demons and start trampling them. Wake up!

Do you need more proof?

Read Paul's prayer for the Ephesians:

I pray also that the eyes of your heart may be enlightened in order that you may know the hope to which He has called you, the riches of His glorious inheritance in the saints, and His incomparably great power for us who believe. That power is like the working of His mighty strength, which He exerted in Christ when He raised Him from the dead and seated Him at His right hand in the heavenly realms, far above all rule and authority, power and dominion, and every title that can be given, not only in the present age but also in the one to come (Ephesians 1:18-21).

What is Paul asking God to reveal to the Ephesians about their inheritance? How much power is available for us? Since, we are seated with Jesus and entrusted with this power, where does that put us?

Paul knew the power he had and he knew that it wasn't only entrusted to him. Here Paul is praying that the Ephesians will get it. He wants the Church to wake up to who she is and what her potential is. He wants the Church to understand her inheritance and walk in it. The passage was written for us today as well. The Church, a long time ago, forgot who she is and where she is seated and that she has power and authority to rule over this world. We still need to wake up to these truths.

There are two times when Jesus states clearly that you can know that the Kingdom of God has come upon you. Matthew 12:28 says, *"But if I drive out demons by the Spirit of God,* ***then the kingdom of God has come upon you"*** (emphasis added). Also, in Luke 11:20 it says, *"But if I drive out demons by the finger of God,* ***then the kingdom of God has come to you."*** (emphasis added).

The reason that Jesus says you can tell that the Kingdom of God is present is that God rules and reigns, and His Kingdom is a greater kingdom, a more powerful kingdom. Demons don't have to flee unless the King is present. When it's time to cast out an evil spirit, you'd better be certain you are in close communion with Christ and that you are walking under His Lordship. The seven sons of Sceva found this out the hard way:

> *Some Jews who went around driving out evil spirits tried to invoke the name of the Lord Jesus over those who were demon-possessed. They would say, "In the name of Jesus, whom Paul preaches, I command you to come out." Seven sons of Sceva, a Jewish chief priest, were doing this. One day the evil spirit answered them, "Jesus I know, and I know about Paul, but who are you?" Then the man who had the evil spirit jumped on them and overpowered them all. He gave them such a beating that they ran out of the house naked and bleeding* (Acts 19:13-16).

In order to drive out demons, one must be walking in the Kingdom of God.

The religious leaders of Jesus' day would have argued this. They accused Jesus Himself of casting out demons by the power of satan in Luke 11. Jesus called them to account and said that it made no sense for satan to cast out satan.

In Matthew 7:22 it says:

> *Many will say to Me on that day, "Lord, Lord, did we not prophesy in Your name, and in Your name drive out demons and perform many miracles?"*

This passage would indicate that it is possible to learn to walk in Kingdom power and not have a relationship with the Lord. Or it could be talking of cult or occult counterfeits. Either way, just because one can or cannot cast out evil spirits does not qualify or disqualify a person. The bulk of Scripture does indicate that this is part of our God-given inheritance and of vital importance to carrying out God's Kingdom agenda. Anyone who is truly in Christ can walk in authority over unclean spirits.

It is evidence that God's Kingdom is real and present when the power of God is present. Many point to the real possibility of counterfeits to say that all power is wrong, and it is amazing how many attribute all power to the devil. That is a very sad delusion that has gripped the Church. It is the same thing Jesus faced when He exercised power in His day. In Matthew 12 and in Luke 11, Jesus was accused of operating under the devil's power. When people don't experience, see, and understand the power of God, they either become humble students or proud antagonists. Which one are you? Are you willing to examine your core beliefs in light of new information, or do you reject anything you don't currently understand?

Jesus wants us to experience His Kingdom power. He wants us to join Him in ruling over this world. Jesus came and died and rose with the purpose of restoring the Kingdom of God. The Kingdom of God is His rule and reign. He trampled satan and even made a public spectacle of him when He triumphed over him at the Cross. In Colossians 2:15 we read this, *"And having disarmed the powers and authorities, He made a public spectacle of them, triumphing over them by the cross."*

There is so much more that we could go into about the Kingdom of God. Jesus went about preaching the Kingdom of God. When He was preaching the Sermon on the Mount, what was He teaching about? Answer: the Kingdom of God. In the Sermon on the Mount, we are learning about the rules of the Kingdom of God. Through His parables, Jesus was speaking about the Kingdom of God. The Kingdom of God is God's reign. There are laws that work in His Kingdom that transcend cultures, time, and the kingdoms of this world.

Everything Jesus said and did was a reflection of life in God's Kingdom. What did Jesus teach about money in God's Kingdom? What did Jesus teach about relationships, forgiveness, and love? What did He teach about priorities? How did Jesus live His life? What were His priorities? What is ministry like for Jesus and His disciples? Is that how we are supposed to live, serve, and love as subjects of His Kingdom? How much power was in operation?

What we consider normal today is not what Christ intended. We don't pay attention to the rules of God's Kingdom. We believe that they are merely good suggestions that the prudish can live by if they want. We believe that grace has allowed us to not have to walk in Christ's Kingdom. After all, Jesus will forgive us, since everyone else is not living according to the Kingdom of God.

What if we studied grace and found out that it really meant something more along the lines of the gifts, strength, and ability to live in God's Kingdom? What if we found out that grace was not an excuse for not walking in the Kingdom, but instead, the enabling for us to walk in the Kingdom? I propose that we have indeed twisted the meaning of grace, or shall I say satan has duped millions (just like he did Eve) into following his definition and standard for Christian living instead of the biblical standard. Just a thought! What does the Bible really say?

Every day we are faced with the choice of which kingdom we will operate under, listen to, and follow. In fact, that choice is faced moment by moment. We see Peter struggling between two kingdoms in Matthew 16. In Matthew 16:16, Peter is declaring Jesus is *"the Christ, the Son of the living God."* Jesus states that God in Heaven revealed this to Peter, that this revelation came from God. In the following paragraph, Peter is seeking to straighten Jesus out by telling Him that they will not let Jesus be crucified. In Matthew 16:23 we read:

Jesus turned and said to Peter, "Get behind Me, Satan! You are a stumbling block to Me; you do not have in mind the things of God, but the things of men."

I don't know about you, but that helps me. We see the apostle Peter as he vacillates between two kingdoms. Christ is constantly urging His followers toward God's Kingdom. If Peter can in one moment be receiving direct revelation from God and in another minute be opening the doorway to allow satan to work in his life, could that happen to you or I? Sure it can. Should we worry? No. That is why we need to walk humbly before God and our fellow man.

It is a moment-by-moment choice. Which Kingdom will I serve? Who will I obey? Will I serve money, power, and fame, which are all a part of satan's kingdom? Or will I serve God's Kingdom and follow the rules of His Kingdom? There are great rewards within the Kingdom of God for those who follow His Kingdom. There are innumerable promises. There are great and dire consequences for not obeying His Kingdom. You can be very religious and not be in Christ's Kingdom. Many of the religious people of Jesus' day never entered into the Kingdom of God.

God's Will Is for Us to Rule as His Sons and Ambassadors!

This means that we have to choose our kingdom—every day, all day! We need to study God's Word if we are going to be able to discern what to do and how to live minute by minute. I believe that every believer needs to study every passage about the Kingdom of God and ask God to give him or her revelation and understanding. This was the message of Jesus and the early Church.

Walk in your inheritance and seek to understand it. We have inherited great power, and yet so few understand, teach, or walk in this facet of their inheritance. We are given the fullness of the deity and are restored to our place of ruling with Christ and having dominion over all of creation. It is time to start trampling the evil one rather than fearing him or subjecting ourselves to his kingdom. Jesus has given us the ability to heal the sick, and yet we are so ignorant today of even what the Bible teaches about healing. (A worthy study is to take every passage that relates to healing and read them in context. Read them again and again and ask Jesus to teach you how to pray for the sick.)

You were created to transform the world. You were created to do what Jesus did. Jesus is what mankind is supposed to be like. He is the only person who has lived God's Kingdom agenda to the fullest. He has restored to us everything we need to join Him in living the Kingdom agenda. Won't you begin the journey of walking out God's Kingdom agenda? Be like Jesus.

Study Questions

1. Before reading *The Jesus Training Manual,* how would you have answered the question, "What was Jesus talking about when he talked about the Kingdom of God?"

   _____

   _____

   _____

2. Why did Jesus talk so much about the Kingdom of God but today we tend to talk so little about it, study it so little, and preach it so seldom?

   _____

   _____

3. This chapter emphasizes the fact that the Kingdom of God means the reign of God. Who was intended to join with God in reigning over this world? What happened?

_____

_____

_____

4. How did Jesus reclaim this world and the rulership from satan? What are some ways that this affects us today?

_____

_____

_____

5. Who gave authority to satan in this world and how? How can we regain authority over satan?

_____

_____

_____

6. Read Ephesians 1:18-21. What is the apostle Paul asking God to reveal to us about our inheritance? How much power is available to us? Since we are seated with Jesus and entrusted with this power, where does this put us?

_____

_____

_____

Closing Thoughts

Try to produce a biblical definition of discipleship that does not include a ministry of healing, casting out demons, and preaching the Kingdom of God. You cannot look at Jesus as your example and do so. Everything Jesus did seemed to revolve around these three things. The Sermon on the Mount was a sermon about the Kingdom of Heaven. Nearly every chapter of the Gospels contains these crucial elements.

Some who read this book will be challenged from a theological perspective to examine God's Word and consider what it means to be a disciple of Jesus in the twenty-first century. My words are not intended to cause you grief or make you feel that your walk with Christ is inferior. When the Lord gently told me that I was not yet a disciple, I was humbled. My prayer is that this book will spur you to truly examine God's Word and be honest. God wants to disciple you.

Others who read this book will gain a sense of hope. As you've read some of the testimonies of changed lives, perhaps you've said, "This is what I've needed all along." Maybe you've been tormented by evil spirits and are on medication because of the voices or things you have seen. Now you've begun to have hope that God can heal you. If you're physically sick, perhaps you've gained hope that God could possibly take away your disease or ailment. Or maybe you've just wondered if God is even out there, and you want to hear His voice and know He's near.

If the paragraph above describes you, I want you to know that there is hope. God can set you free. He can heal you. He wants to speak to you, and He wants you to hear His voice. It can be very frustrating if you belong to a church that doesn't believe in this or that teaches you to avoid anyone who does. I would never advise that you leave your church, but make sure to hold God's Word above what your denomination teaches. It's best that you find someone who's been discipled by Jesus and who knows how to cast out evil spirits and pray for the sick for healing.

If you don't know anyone like this, hope is not lost. There are other methods God can use. There are great books on these subjects, many of which I have mentioned in the reading list at the back of this book. Each book I recommend has a solid biblical foundation and can be helpful. The problem with books is that you may understand a concept but not know how to put it into practice. Jesus taught "live and in person." The disciples watched Him and listened.

My wife and I, along with the Operation Light Force team, have developed and are developing resources in each of the areas of discipleship discussed in this book.

Operation Light Force holds Freedom Conferences and Lord, Disciple Me conferences, Lord, Heal Me conferences, as well as prayer ministry skills training conferences. God has used these to transform many people's lives. These conferences, held in homes of hungry disciples, at local churches, and even conference halls involve teaching, then ministry for those persons attending. People are set free from depression, fears, addictions, hatred, rage, and other forms of bondage. The testimonies following these conferences are extremely encouraging—and God has used this ministry to produce fruit in churches of many different denominations.

We also offer Five-Day Intensive Care ministry where people come for one week of intensive ministry. The level of transformation that people experience is always amazing. One executive flew in last week because of an addiction to prescription drugs. God healed him from more than that. People fly in from all over who have been to treatment centers and hospitals with all kinds of physical, emotional, and mental illnesses. God has brought healing to so many.

My earnest prayer is that God will raise up New Testament disciples by the millions. We at Operation Light Force are asking Him to provide a training center where disciples can be trained by the thousands. With each disciple, hundreds of people will be set free, healed, and saved in miraculous and powerful ways.

APPENDIX A

Resources

The following is a list of recommended reading. These books will be useful tools in helping you become victorious and effective as a disciple of Jesus Christ. It is God's will that you develop and grow as a disciple. Here are the books that helped me. Don't be scared off by some of the titles. This is the stuff Jesus taught to 12 ordinary guys.

Anderson, Neil T. *The Bondage Breaker*. Eugene, Oregon: Harvest House Publishers, 1990.

Anacondia, Carlos. *Listen to Me Satan*. Nashville: Creation House, 1998.

Blackaby, Henry T., and Claude V. King. *Experiencing God*. Nashville, TN: Lifeway Press, 1990.

Eldredge, John. *Waking the Dead*. Nashville: Thomas Nelson Publishers, 2003.

Horrobin, Peter. *Healing Through Deliverance 1*. Michigan: Chosen Books Publishing Co., 2003.

Horrobin, Peter. *Healing Through Deliverance 2*. Michigan: Chosen Books Publishing Co., 2003.

Larson, Bob. *Shock Talk*. Florida: Thomas Nelson Publishers, 2001.

Penn Lewis, Jesse. *War on the Saints*. Pennsylvania: Christian Literature Crusade, 1993.

Prince, Derek. *They Shall Expel Demons*. Michigan: Chosen Books Publishing Co., 1998.

Wimber, John, with Kevin Springer. *Power Healing*. San Francisco: Harper Collins, 1987.

APPENDIX B[1]

Healing in Scriptures

Here is an extensive list of passages in the Bible that contain some element of teaching about healing. If you will read each of these passages in its context, you will begin to gain a more thorough understanding of what God's Word teaches us concerning healing. Whatever you have been taught and believe must be examined in light of what God's Word teaches us. Study to show yourself approved of God.

Old Testament Passages

Genesis 20:17
Exodus 15
Numbers 12:13
Deuteronomy 28
Deuteronomy 32:39
1 Samuel 6:3
2 Kings 2:21
2 Kings 5
2 Kings 20
2 Chronicles 7:14
2 Chronicles 30:20

Healing in Poetry Books

Psalm 6:2
Psalm 30:2
Psalm 38:3
Psalm 41:3
Psalm 103:3
Psalm 107:20
Psalm 147:3
Proverbs 3:7-8
Proverbs 4:20-22
Proverbs 12:18
Proverbs 13:17
Proverbs 15:30
Proverbs 16:24
Ecclesiastes 3:3

Healing in the Prophets

Isaiah 6:10
Isaiah 19:22
Isaiah 30:26
Isaiah 53:4-6
Isaiah 57:17-19
Isaiah 58:8
Isaiah 61:1
Jeremiah 3:22
Jeremiah 6:14
Jeremiah 8:11
Jeremiah 8:15
Jeremiah 8:22
Jeremiah 14:19
Jeremiah 17:14
Jeremiah 30:13
Jeremiah 30:17
Jeremiah 33:6

Jeremiah 51:8
Jeremiah 51:9
Ezekiel 34:2-4

Healing Water Flows From God's Temple

Ezekiel 47:8
Hosea 6:1

Healing of Nations and Land

Ezekiel 47:11
Hosea 5:13
Hosea 7:1
Hosea 11:3
Hosea 14:4

Old Testament Words for Healing

Rapha—*raw-faw'*—Used in the King James Version of the Bible 67 times and translated as: "heal" (57), "physician" (5), "cure" (1), "repaired" (1), misc (3).

To heal, make healthful

1. To heal—of God, healer, physician (of men), of hurts of nations involving restored favor, of individual distresses

2. To be healed—literal (of persons), of water, pottery, of national hurts, of personal distress

3. To heal—literal, of national defects or hurts

4. In order to get healed (infinitive)

Marpe—*mar-pay'*—Translated in the King James 16 times as: "health" (5), "healing" (3), "remedy" (3), "incurable" (1), "cure" (1), "sound" (1), "wholesome" (1), "yielding" (1).

Health, healing, cure

Riph'uwth—*rif-ooth'*—Translated in the King James as "health" (1).

Healing

New Testament Passages

Jesus' Ministry Was Healing

Matthew 4:23
Matthew 8:7
Matthew 8:13
Matthew 8:16
Matthew 9:35
Matthew 12:10
Matthew 12:15
Matthew 12:22
Matthew 14:14
Matthew 15:28
Matthew 15:30
Matthew 19:2
Matthew 21:14
Mark 1:34
Mark 3:2
Mark 3:10
Mark 3:15
Mark 5:23
Mark 5:29
Mark 5:34
Mark 6:5
Luke 4:18
Luke 4:23
Luke 4:40

Luke 5:15
Luke 5:17
Luke 6:7
Luke 6:17
Luke 6:18
Luke 7:3
Luke 7:7
Luke 8:2
Luke 8:36
Luke 8:43
Luke 8:47
Luke 9:11
Luke 9:42
Luke 13:14
Luke 14:3
Luke 14:4
Luke 17:15
Luke 22:51
John 4:47
John 5:13
John 12:40

Disciples and 72 Commissioned to Do as Jesus Did

Matthew 10:1
Matthew 10:8
Mark 6:7
Luke 9:2
Luke 9:6
Luke 10:9

Healing in Acts

Acts 3:11
Acts 4:14
Acts 4:22

Acts 4:30

Acts 5:16

Acts 8:7

Acts 9:34

Acts 10:38

Acts 14:9

Acts 28:8

Acts 28:27

Healing in the Epistles

1 Corinthians 12:9

1 Corinthians 12:28

1 Corinthians 12:30

Hebrews 12:13

James 5:16

1 Peter 2:24

3 John 1:2

Healing in Revelation

Revelation 22:2

New Testament Words for Healing

Therapeuo—*ther-ap-yoo'-o*—Translated in the King James 44 times as: "heal" (38), "cure" (5), "worship" (1).

1. To serve, do service

2. To heal, cure, restore to health

Sozo—*sode'-zo*—Translated in the King James 110 times as: "save" (93), "make whole" (9), "heal" (3), "be whole" (2), misc (3).

To save, keep safe and sound, to rescue from danger or destruction.

1. One (from injury or peril) (to save a suffering one [from perishing], i.e., one suffering from disease, to make well, heal, restore to health, to preserve one who is in danger of destruction, to save or rescue)

2. To save in the technical biblical sense (negatively—to deliver from the penalties of the Messianic judgment, to save from the evils that obstruct the reception of the Messianic deliverance)

Iaomai—*ee-ah'-om-ahee*—Translated in the King James 28 times as: "heal" (26), "make whole" (2).

1. To cure, heal

2. To make whole (to free from errors and sins, to bring about [one's] salvation)

Diasozo—*dee-as-odze'-o*—Translated in the King James 8 times as: "escape" (2), "save" (2), "make perfectly whole" (1), "escape safe" (1), "bring safe" (1), "heal" (1).

1. To preserve through danger, to bring safely through (to save, i.e., cure one who is sick, bring him through)

2. To save, keep from perishing

3. To save out of danger, rescue

Endnote

1. Word definitions throughout Appendix B are from the Online Bible; http://www.kingjamesbibleonline.org/; accessed October 20, 2010.

APPENDIX C

Open Door List

The following is a great practical guide to finding significant personal healing. This personal inventory can be done and strongholds can be broken from an individual's life. Write your answers to the open doors listed below on a separate piece of paper. When you are finished with the proclamations, destroy the list as a symbol of your freedom.

Opening prayer:

Lord, thank You that Your desire is to destroy the work the evil one has wrought in my life. Please search me and know me in the following areas and bring to my awareness in my heart and mind anything that stands in the way of my relationship with You. Thank You, in Jesus' name, amen.

1. UNFORGIVENESS

List all people or groups of people (churches, organizations, races, etc.) from childhood to the present you have or have ever had any unforgiveness or bitterness or resentment (dead or alive) toward or that you have wrongly judged, condemned, or cursed.

PROCLAMATION OF FORGIVENESS: Lord, thank You for for-giving me. Now, I want to confess that I have not loved, but have resented, certain people and have unforgiveness and condemnation in my heart. Lord, I call upon You to help me to forgive even as You have forgiven me. Now, knowing that I cannot be forgiven unless I forgive, and knowing that if I curse what You have blessed, that curse falls back on me, I choose to forgive and release all judgments and curses against [call out every person or group of people the Lord put in your mind]. Now, I forgive and accept myself in the name of Jesus. In place of this unforgiveness and resentment, fill me with a renewed love for You and fill me with Your Holy Spirit of love and blessing toward these indi-viduals and groups, and since faith without works is dead, give me clear direction as to how I can actively love and bless these people.

2. OCCULT PRACTICES

List all involvement you have had with the occult, including things like: Ouija boards, séances, witchcraft, astrology, secret societies such as Freemasonry, books read involving witchcraft, and games played related to anything occult.

PROCLAMATION FOR OCCULT CONFESSION: Lord Jesus, I confess seeking from satan and his kingdom the help that should have come from God almighty. I confess as sin [name all occult sins] and even those I do not remember. Lord, I repent and renounce these sins, and ask You to forgive me. [You must renounce each god or each oath made in Freemasonry.] In the name of Jesus, I now close the door to all occult practices. Satan, I renounce you and all your works in my life, in the name of Jesus Christ of Nazareth, and I close all the doors of my life to the entry points you previously gained through my involvement in the occult. Enemy, I speak out, in the name of Jesus who defeated you at Calvary, that you no longer have any right to trouble me on these specific issues—which have now been confessed, repented of, and forgiven, and from which I have been cleansed by the shed blood of the Lord Jesus Christ. Lord, I submit my life totally and completely to You. Now fill me with the Holy Spirit.

3. SEXUAL SIN

List all people you have been sexually involved with outside of marriage (example: fornication, adultery, rape, molestation, incest, homosexuality/lesbianism, bestiality). Even list your spouse if you came together sexually prior to marriage.

> *PROCLAMATION TO BE SET FREE FROM SEXUAL SIN: Thank You, Jesus, for dying on the Cross, that I might be forgiven. I confess all my sexual sin. I invite You, Jesus, to be Lord of my life, especially my sexuality. And I ask You to set me free from everyone I have had relations with in an ungodly way. I recognize this is sin and I do not want to continue in these relationships. [Name each relationship out loud that you listed.] I speak to any spirit in satan's kingdom that has come into me through these sexual relationships and I break that legal tie and cast you out by the authority I have in Jesus Christ. You have no further right in my spirit, soul, and body, and I order you to leave me now, in the name of Jesus. Lord, fill me now with Your Holy Spirit of love, purity, holiness, and Holy Spirit, empower me to keep my eyes and heart focused on Jesus, not my flesh. I now reckon myself dead to sin and alive to Christ and commit, with Holy Spirit power, my body as an instrument of righteousness.*

4. SOUL TIES

List all people (dead or alive) who have had an ungodly control over you such as: your mother, father, stepparents, spouse, grandparents, spirit guides, aborted babies, hypnotists, ex-spouse, brothers/sisters (full or step), children (full, step, adopted, foster), etc. Also include names from number three above, sexual partners. Also include anyone you have had a lustful relationship with or an "affair of the heart" between you and another. (This can be as simple as someone you "caught eyes with" and you could "sense" immediately there was something between you, even if nothing else ever happened. It could result from an "extended" look at another even if nothing else ever happened.) List any family members who have died and whose negative traits have been attributed to you. Also, list any experiences with excessive grief (longer than one year), loneliness, or rejection (including miscarriages and abortions).

PROCLAMATION BREAKING UNGODLY SOUL TIES: Thank You, Jesus, for dying that I might be set free. I invite You, Lord Jesus, to be Lord of my life, and I ask You to set me free. I confess and repent of my sin with [name out loud everyone on list]. I forgive and loose in the freedom of my forgiveness those with whom I have ungodly soul ties. I now break and renounce any ungodly soul ties with [name out loud everyone on list]. I now use the authority I have in Jesus Christ and break and renounce these ungodly soul ties and command any demonic spirits that entered me through these relationships to leave me now. Lord, fill me with Your Holy Spirit of love, blessing, honor, and purity for my present and future relationships. Holy Spirit, also guard my heart and my mind and my eyes from this moment forward. Everything that I have lost in that relationship [specific persons] must be returned to me, in Jesus' name.

5. COVENANTS, VOWS, AND CURSES

List all broken covenants and vows of the past. This may include marriages, bankruptcy, church membership, etc., or curses spoken over your life by friends, parents, family, self, or others. Also list any covenants or vows any family members have made concerning you (such as done in fraternal orders or secret societies like the Freemasons).

PROCLAMATION ON BROKEN COVENANTS/VOWS CON-FESSION: Lord Jesus, I confess that I have broken covenant/vows with You. I recognize this is sin and I ask You, Lord, to forgive me now for breaking these between You and [name each one on list]. I now use my authority I have in Jesus Christ and break any curses this has brought upon me and order every spirit in satan's kingdom to leave me now. I also break every curse spoken over me through any involvement in any fraternal order or Freemasonry. Lord, fill me with Your Holy Spirit in these areas vacated by the enemy.

6. TRAUMATIC EVENTS, ABUSE, HURTS, AND REJECTIONS

(Sexual, Verbal, Emotional, Psychological, Abandonment)—Name all people or groups who have rejected you, abused you, or hurt you. List all traumatic events (e.g., accidents, injuries).

PROCLAMATION REGARDING TRAUMATIC EVENTS, ABUSE, HURTS, AND REJECTIONS: Father, I confess that, as a result of being hurt, I have allowed myself to hold anger, resentment, and bitterness in my heart against [insert here the names of individuals]. I acknowledge this as sin, and I now repent and turn from it. I ask that You will forgive me and cleanse me. I also know that this has resulted in my defiling others through gossip or hurtful talk. Please forgive me and cleanse me for defiling [name all people you have defiled in this way]. I break the hold the enemy has on me as a result of this and command the enemy to leave me now through the authority of Jesus' name. Lord, fill me with the Holy Spirit of love and blessing in these areas and for these people, showing me any work of faith I must now do as led by Your Spirit. Everything that I have lost in that event [name specific event] must be returned to me, in Jesus' name.

7. SOME ALTERNATIVE MEDICAL PRACTICES

List all alternative medical practices, such as hypnosis, acupuncture, aromatherapy, crystal therapy, faith healers, guided imagery, new age medicine, past lives therapy, psychic healers, etc.

PROCLAMATION REGARDING ALTERNATIVE MEDICAL PRACTICES: Lord, I confess as sin [name out loud everything listed above] and repent of them. I break any legal ground the enemy has taken in these areas and break all assignments of the enemy over my life in these areas. I close the open doors by the authority of Jesus' name and His shed blood. I ask now, Lord, to be filled with the Spirit, and I commit, with Your power, to trust in Christ and Christ alone for every area and circumstance of my life, now and forever.

8. GENERATIONAL CURSES

List abuse, prejudice, occult practices, sexual immorality, divorce, emotional death (Masonic), alcoholism, or any other pattern noted to be passed down generational lines.

PROCLAMATION: Lord, I agree with You and confess as sin [name out loud known generational sin]. I choose to forgive [name persons] for these sins and ask for Your forgiveness for their sin and my part in it. I break these curses over myself and my family and succeeding generations in Jesus' name.

[The preceding material is taken from Steve Minter as adapted from Paul and Claire Hollis of New Beginnings, and was used by permission.]

APPENDIX D

In His Own Words

Jeff, whose story is told in Chapter 14, sent me this testimony written in his own words:

At first I thought I should keep this short, but in order for you to get the whole picture on the amazing work God has done in my life, I have to tell you all the details. I'm not sure what your beliefs are as far as God is concerned, but it takes a very strong and determined person to defeat emotional problems and/or addictions without God. In my case, God pulled me out of the hole that I had dug for myself in a matter of hours. I want you to know I greatly appreciate your time in reading this letter, and I pray that it may in some way help you on your path to a better and more meaningful life.

It really started to get bad about one year ago. I had been using drugs and alcohol for quite some time. It was all for fun and recreation at first, but over time, I realized that I was only using to get a release from the drudgery my life had become. I had always had an anger problem, and I had been struggling with depression since I was 14 years old. I decided to rebel and live life my way, which was when these problems began to grow within me.

Everything seemed to be going OK until I attended a music festival. During a three-day festival, I used narcotics continually. On Saturday night, I was under the influence of alcohol, marijuana, LSD, and ecstasy. As you can imagine, I was blasted. Then something happened that I believe started the downfall in my life. I didn't pay much attention to this event until after I received healing and forgiveness from Jesus. As I was in the midst of the crowd watching a music group called "Disturbed" on stage, I suddenly passed out and hit the ground. I do not remember falling or how long I was out, but I still remember the fear I felt. As I was out, I saw my face surrounded by darkness, as though I was looking in a mirror. I continued to look as all of my skin and muscles melted off of my face and all that remained was my skull. I was freaked. I could feel fear surrounding me and penetrating me like never before. I could not shake the vision. Then I saw my skull transform into the face of a black demon with glowing red eyes and a sly smirk on his face. Now I understand that I was under the major influence of drugs, but it was not the first time I had been under that influence. At first I thought it was just a drug-induced hallucination, but even if it was, that does not explain the consuming sense of fear that entered me. As I look back on my life, I now know that this was the moment that my life began to fall apart.

Soon after that weekend concert, I was fired because of a failed drug screening. I got another job quickly, but it did not take long for my anger to get the best of me. I ended up quitting because I was mad about certain things that were going on. Looking back, that was a very stupid mistake on my part. But my pride and anger would not allow me to stay. At that time, my son, Collin, was living with me, and my responsibilities were mounting. I had stopped hanging out with my "drug buddies" because I no longer worked with them, and I didn't want their influence around Collin. With all these things changing in my life, I still held on to my addictions more than ever before. I wasn't working, so I would take Collin to school and come home and spend all day getting high. My anger with my situation and the world around me would not even allow me to look for another job. I was completely torn on the inside. On one hand, I knew I had responsibilities to take care of, but on the other, my selfish pride and my growing depression were causing me to stay right where I was.

It got to the point where I would only leave the house when I had to (driving Collin back and forth to school, going shopping, and buying drugs). I was isolating myself from everything and everybody around me. My depression thickened. During this time, my son's mother, Sharon, and I were going through a custody battle. And although I was a complete wreck inside, I was able to deceive people into thinking I was OK. I had become a "master" of the art of lying. Anything I could say or do to keep my addiction a secret, that is what I did.

There came a point when I just could not take the pressure anymore. The fight for Collin was driving me crazy. Even though my heart and mind were totally screwed up, the one thing I was always sure about was that I loved Collin. But I had a choice to make. Was I going to try to clean up and provide for my son, or would I continue to be selfish and hardhearted and do things my way? One day I got so angry at the situation that I just gave up and handed custody over to Sharon. At the time, I just wanted out of all the stress. Once again, I chose to run from my problems instead of facing them head on.

After that I really was alone. I started to have strong feelings of hatred toward myself. What kind of person would choose a drug over his own son? How could I be so selfish? When would all of this pain go away?

No matter how hard I tried to run, my pain would just continue to get bigger and bigger.

I was lonely, depressed, angry, and sad while I sat at the bottom of my downward spiral. I started giving serious thought to suicide, because at the time I believed it was the only way to get away from the anguish I felt in my soul. I spent every bit of my savings on drugs. I was high from the moment I woke up until the time I would go to bed. I no longer knew what it felt like to be sober. At first the drugs would make the pain go away and I would only feel numb, but in the long run they only intensified my pain. I had lost the trust of everyone around me, including my parents and my brother Steve, because of my lying and uselessness. But what did I do? I continued to turn my back on everyone who cared about me and I continued to wallow in my own self-pity.

I still remember one day I took my brother's gun out of his safe and stood in front of the mirror with it against my temple. While I was smiling at the thought of finally stopping the hurt, there was that very subtle voice in the back of my head that said, "If you do this, your soul will be in hell, and that is where the real suffering will begin." I couldn't do it. I wanted to, but I just couldn't. This made me even crazier.

Meanwhile my parents were urging me to see a psychologist—but I refused. My attitude was that I knew that I had gotten myself into this mess and I did not want help from anybody. In my mind I did not deserve help. I felt that it would be a waste of time for anybody to help me because I knew deep down that their help wouldn't do any good until I was willing to help myself. A couple of days later (once I had completely run out of money), I tried to commit suicide by eating about half a bottle of Excedrin. I thought, *At least this way I will go while I am sleeping.*

Today I realize that had it not been for God pulling me through that night, I would not be alive today. I should not have lived to see morning. I understand now that God had a reason to pull me through and that He has a plan for my life. Not long after that night, I had to move back to my parents' house because my brother no longer wanted me living with him and mooching off of him. He was paying all the bills and was fed up with my behavior. I was not happy about this at all, but I understood why Steve felt the way he did. I also did not want to move back to my parents' house, but I really had no other choice.

During this time of my downfall, I was spending a lot of time reading and researching different faiths (religions). As you can imagine, I had a lot of free time on my hands. My main motivation behind my search was to find some way to disprove the Christian faith. During my life, I had always been told how Christians were supposed to live and act. But as I grew older, I noticed that most of the Christians I knew were a bunch of hypocrites. That is when I decided I didn't want anything to do with a religion that was so weak that it could not reach the people who were involved in it. Now I realize that it really has nothing to do with the other people in church or the religion itself—it's because people are sinners and religion is a man-made institution. Even as hard as I tried to believe otherwise, I could not shake the feeling that Jesus was the only way to freedom.

One night while I was sleeping, something strange happened. Obviously I had no idea what happened until my stepfather told me the next morning, because I was sound asleep. My stepfather was faithfully praying for me while standing outside the door to my bedroom. While he anointed my door with oil, he spoke out against satan's control over me. Then he moved to the living room and anointed the wall where I was sleeping just on the other side. After doing so, I let out a tremendously loud scream that scared everyone else in the home. The strange thing is that I did not hear or remember anything. I now know that was the time when satan was cut off from controlling my thoughts, and he was not happy about it. You see, when my stepdad stood up in Jesus' name against satan, he fled because he knew that his strength could not compare to Jesus'. Remember, First John 4:3-4 reads:

> But every spirit that does not acknowledge Jesus is not from God. This is the spirit of the antichrist, which you have heard is coming and even now is already in the world. You, dear children, are from God and have overcome them, because the one who is in you is greater than the one who is in the world.

I will explain more about this later. The next day, after my mind had been loosed, I began my journey to Jesus and total freedom.

That morning I decided to meet with a man named Richard Mull. He had spent his whole life in the church and in ministry. He spent seven years earning his master's of divinity, which includes degrees in theology and the Bible. I wanted to meet with him so that I could discuss with him what I thought were contradictions in the Bible. After he explained the answers to my questions, he told me something that shocked me. He said that all of the theological degrees and knowledge meant nothing to him. He explained that even after earning them, he still did not feel the holy love and power of God that the Bible talks about. He told me that the most important aspect of our faith is to have a close personal relationship with God.

I do not know how familiar you are with deliverance, but Richard offered to meet with me another time to pray deliverance with me. I was very hesitant about the idea. We sat for about 30 minutes before I agreed. I thought to myself, *I always try to be open-minded about everything, except the idea that Christianity might be true. Why not just give it a shot and see what happens?* I knew that I needed something to happen. I needed some kind of healing before I ended up in a psychiatric ward. It was worth a try.

Two days later when I went to Richard's house, I was very nervous and I almost did not show up because I felt afraid. The unusual thing is that the moment I stepped into his office I felt an overwhelming sense of comfort. After explaining to me what we were going to do, he and his friend, Victor, began to pray. They were praying more powerfully than I had ever seen in my life. They asked in faith for the Holy Spirit to come down and give them discernment about the strongholds and emotional problems I had. At this point, I was starting to think that I had made a big mistake by going there. I almost got up and walked out.

After praying, they began to stand strongly in the name of Jesus, and they claimed authority over the evil spirits that were within me. They began to speak against the spirits of anger, depression, rejection, hatred, addiction, and double-mindedness, among others. At this point, I was crying and coughing like crazy. My entire body was involuntarily shaking and twitching. They came against suicide, envy, inferiority, perfection, and loneliness as they demanded the evil spirits leave in the name of Jesus. After speaking over rejection, Richard told me that my father never meant to make me feel rejected but he just didn't know how to show love to me.

The funny thing is, Richard has never met my dad and had no idea what my relationship with him was like.

Then he said something that really freaked me out. He told me that God has forgiven me for cursing Him and telling Him that I never wanted anything to do with Him again. The strange thing about this is that a couple of months earlier, I had lain in my bed at my old home with the door closed, and I had spent about ten minutes yelling and cursing at God. I told Him that I hated Him and that I wanted Him out of my life and my mind forever. When Richard said these things, I really lost it. I was broken to the point where I could hardly stay conscious. I thought, *How does this guy know these things? I was alone in my home when I said these things to God! I've never told anyone about that moment in my life. Is God using this man to speak forgiveness to me for something only He knows about? That is the only explanation! God is speaking to me through this man! These things do not happen in real life!*

We got to the point where I felt as though they had spoken out all of the evil spirits that had control over my life. But something still didn't feel right. I did feel like a large amount of weight had been lifted off of my soul, but I knew that there was something lingering. I heard a very faint snickering in the back of my head that was whispering, "I'm still here." For a moment I thought, *What was that!*

Then Richard looked at me and asked me, "What is left? There is still something holding on, and it is strong. Do you know what it is?" I took some time to think and I couldn't come up with an answer. After about five minutes or so, a picture entered my mind. With my eyes closed I saw a cross surrounded in darkness. I told them, "You're not going to believe this, but all I can see is a cross." They told me to focus and see what else came to mind. The next thing I knew, in my mind I was seeing a view of the church building that I attended as I grew up. On the front of the church there had been a large cross facing the street so that it was the first thing you would see as you entered the parking lot.

After telling Richard and Victor what I was seeing, they began to come against the evil spirit of religion. When they did so, I felt every muscle in my body become tense and my feet felt like they were glued to the floor. You see, my bitterness and animosity toward church and religion had become the driving force behind all of the other problems in my life. Man-made religion, and my hatred toward it, was the root of my pain. It is what gave the enemy the right to bring strongholds and torment into my life. It took longer for the spirit of religion to loose me than any other that had me in their grips. It was stronger and more deeply rooted than depression, anger, addiction, suicide, and rejection. It was hard for me to believe that something that is supposed to be so good could be tainted by man to the point where it was the foundation of satan's "house" inside me.

Once the evil spirit of religion left me I felt an overwhelming sense of peace and freedom that I had never felt before. I felt a "high" that no drug had ever given me. I had tried every drug that the world has to offer so that I could escape my problems and feel total freedom, but none of them could compare with the freedom that God gave to me on that day.

God came to me and swept me clean of all the strongholds and filled me with His Holy Spirit. For the first time in a long time, I felt hope, not only for my life, but for everything around me. I felt as though I was finally set loose from the straitjacket that this world had put me in. I felt like a child again, free from all of the emotional pain that had been built up in me throughout my life. I would say the most amazing thing is that from that day forward, I have never felt depression, anger, or hatred in my heart. The only time that drugs even enter my thoughts are when I am telling my testimony to others. God completely delivered me from all of these things in a matter of three hours!

I understand that it is hard for most people today to believe that God works this strongly in the lives of others who completely submit themselves to Him. Most of us have been taught that God doesn't do these things in the modern day. We are brought up believing that Jesus' practice of healing and casting out demons was something that only happened during the lives of the disciples. But let me tell you that I experienced firsthand the healing of Jesus. And furthermore, anyone who is willing to submit themselves completely to the power of God will also experience a freedom like they have never felt before.

Why do most Christians limit the strength and power of the Almighty God? He is capable of anything. And I will tell you, He continues to work miracles of healing and deliverance today. God has never stopped doing these things. The only reason we have not seen them happen today is because we have not believed that He has the power to do them. I have seen God do some powerful things in the past year and will continue to see these things because I know that He wants the world to see Him. God wants us to wake up and smell the coffee. Why continue to live in the bondage of emotional and sociological strongholds if you don't have to? The Lord is waiting for us to realize His healing strength. He is reaching out for us. All we have to do is go to Him in faith and take His hand. With God, all things are possible.

May God Bless You All,

Jeff

P.S. If there is anybody you know that you think could benefit from hearing my story, please do not hesitate to share it with them.

Notes

Notes

Notes

Notes

Notes

Notes

Notes

Notes

More About Richard Mull

Richard Mull
President
Operation Light Force

813-817-1651

rmull@operationlightforce.com
www.operationlightforce.com
www.lightforceinstitute.com

Other Books by Richard Mull

Lord, Heal Me

The 40-Day Revolution

IN THE RIGHT HANDS, THIS BOOK WILL CHANGE LIVES!

Most of the people who need this message will not be looking for this book. To change their lives, you need to put a copy of this book in their hands.

> *But others (seeds) fell into good ground, and brought forth fruit, some a hundred-fold, some sixty-fold, some thirty-fold* (Matthew 13:8).

Our ministry is constantly seeking methods to find the good ground, the people who need this anointed message to change their lives. Will you help us reach these people?

> *Remember this—a farmer who plants only a few seeds will get a small crop. But the one who plants generously will get a generous crop* (2 Corinthians 9:6).

EXTEND THIS MINISTRY BY SOWING
3 BOOKS, 5 BOOKS, 10 BOOKS, OR MORE TODAY,
· AND BECOME A LIFE CHANGER!

Thank you,

Don Nori Sr., Publisher
Destiny Image
Since 1982